Theology Today

GENERAL EDITOR:

EDWARD YARNOLD, S. J.

No. 3

The Theology of Faith

BY

JOHN COVENTRY, S. J.

THE MERCIER PRESS

4 BRIDGE STREET CORK

ACKNOWLEDGEMENTS

The Scripture quotations in the publication are from the *Revised Standard Version of the Bible* copyrighted 1946 and 1952 by the Division of Christian Education of the National Council of the Churches of Christ in the U.S.A. and used by permission; the quotations from *The Documents of Vatican II* (ed. W. M. Abbott, S. J.) are printed by kind permission of the America Press and Geoffrey Chapman, London.

ABBREVIATIONS

PG   J. P. Migne: *Patrologia Graeca.*
PL   J. P. Migne: *Patrologia Latina.*
Dz   H. Denzinger & A. Schönmetzer,
   *Enchiridion Symbolorum, Definitionum
   et Declarationum* (33rd edit., Barcelona etc., 1965).

CONTENTS

PREFACE

The 'Theology Today' Series began with the study of the subject of all theology, the Incarnate Christ. The second volume discussed revelation, which is the Father's word spoken by Christ. Man's response to revelation is faith. Faith, then, is the subject of this, the third book in the series.

Just as revelation is not the publication by God of a series of true propositions, but is a person, Christ, the self-manifestation of the Father, so too faith is not primarily the acceptance of a series of guaranteed propositions, but is the acceptance of a person, Christ.

What then is the connection between faith in Christ and faith in the dogmas of the Church? This is the theme of Fr. Coventry's book.

E. J. Yarnold, S.J.

CHAPTER 1

OUTLINE

1. *Faith in Christ*

The main contention of this book is a simple one: that faith is primarily in Christ, and not in doctrines; in God presenting himself for recognition as a person, and not in any series of doctrinal statements or propositions, which we are asked to believe. These are secondary, and adherence to them can only be understood in the context of adherence to Christ. This, it will be maintained, is the key to solve the puzzles, and the detergent to wash away all the intricacy of complication that has been spun about the analysis and understanding of faith.

This is surely the characteristic situation in the gospels. Our Lord asks for faith in himself. When he said, 'Your faith has made you well' (Lk 17.19; 18.42), he was not referring to any acceptance of propositions, but to a faith in himself, deeper than mere faith in his healing powers, which he could discern in the sufferers who came to him. The moment of faith came for Peter in the miraculous haul of fish, when he recognised who Christ was: 'He fell down at Jesus' knees, saying, "Depart from me, for I am a sinful man, O Lord"' (Lk 5.8). Our Lord did not say to Thomas, 'Blessed are they who have first carefully sifted all the evidence', but, on the contrary, 'Blessed are those who have not seen and yet believe' (Jn 20.29) – a challenging passage, if we are accustomed to think that our faith must be grounded on a solid construct of human argument, and one to return to.

Faith and revelation are correlative terms, and can only be understood in view of each other. Faith is man's response to revelation. So what, basically, *is* revelation?

The only full answer is that revelation is Christ. God cannot, as it were, hand himself over to man, show himself to man, just as he is in himself. He has to put himself into human terms for us to understand. He expressed himself in human terms (spoke) 'of old to our fathers by the prophets; but in these last days he has spoken to us by a Son... (who) bears the very stamp of his nature' (Heb 1.1-3). Christ, the incarnation, is God's Last Word. He has expressed himself fully and definitively in human terms. There could not be anything more to say – and this is the basis of the doctrine that the deposit of faith closed with the death of the last apostle.

It is not just a question of what Our Lord *said* (as if the true gospel message could not be put forward, until we had unearthed from the available accounts the 'original message of Jesus'), but primarily of what he *was* – a divine person expressing himself humanly, not only in word, but in gesture and mannerism and deed, above all in his life, death and resurrection. It is only through this whole complex of living, outwardly manifested, that we can 'get at', get to know, understand, evaluate, establish a personal relationship with, any person. Some Christian traditions have tended to limit 'the Word of God' too exclusively to the spoken word, recorded in Scripture. But the self-expression of God in human terms is God's whole historical intervention in the history of his chosen people, and his definitive historical intervention in the incarnation.

> To see Jesus is to see his Father (Jn 14.9). For this reason Jesus perfected revelation by fulfilling it through his whole work of making himself present and manifesting himself: through his words and deeds, his signs and wonders, but especially through his death and glorious resurrection from the dead and final sending of the Spirit of truth. (Vatican II, *Const. on Divine Revelation*, n. 4.)

One might sum it up by saying that revelation considered actively, as God's activity of revealing himself, is Christ – not appearing suddenly or unheralded, but as the centre of God's self-expressing intervention in history, the centre of salvation history. Revelation considered passively, or revelation received, is the total impact of Christ (and not just of what he said) on men, and principally on the apostles and other eye-witnesses.

Faith is the correlative of revelation. Those who believed, when confronted with Christ's life, death and resurrection, were those who recognised that it was God who confronted them. This is faith. We will discuss and analyse it further, but this is what it essentially is: not a process of argument resulting in a conclusion; not the acceptance of a proposition; but a religious experience, sometimes sudden and overwhelming, that you are confronted with God, to which you may well respond by saying, 'depart from me for I am a sinful man, O Lord'.

The matter may be illustrated by comparison and contrast with human faith. You have a bit of money to invest, and your brother-in-law, who is a stockbroker, advises you where to place it. Now, you have no difficulty in knowing who it is that is addressing you: it is your brother-in-law. And consequently you can be quite confident that he is on your side, and is not trying to cheat you for some devious purposes of his own. So the whole question about putting faith in him rests on whether he has correctly diagnosed the state of the market, whether what he says is true. But in divine faith the factors are reversed. *If* it is God speaking to you, then both his good will and the truth of what he says are certain. The whole problem will be to be sure that it is God speaking.

The 'gift of faith' is the grace given by God to recognise that it is in truth he that is confronting you, speaking.

We may clarify the situation further by quite simply looking at the problem from God's angle. He cannot present himself to man 'just as he is'. So (like any person making himself felt and understood) he must give external signs: they are signs of his *message*, what he wants to say; and they are signs that it is *his* message, that it is he who is addressing man. But to this external revelation there must be coupled the gift and interior action of his Spirit (sometimes called internal revelation), namely the power to recognise that it is in truth his message.

Thus it can be seen that for the origin of faith two elements are necessary, an external and an internal. Neither element is sufficient without the other. The same evidence, the external signs, may well be spread before many: but only those will believe who have the power to recognise God presenting himself in these signs, God confronting them. Nor, conversely, is faith simply a matter of interior inspiration (as some seem to imagine), a peculiar 'religious experience' divorced from consideration of evidence: it is the power to see what the evidence is evidence of.

Thus faith is correctly explained as knowledge through signs, or, perhaps better, a personal relation established through signs. There must be external signs, by which God conveys himself in his message. But one does not know a sign *as* a sign, until one knows what it is a sign *of*: present a musical score to a savage, and it will be only a meaningless jumble of marks; some kind of insight based on education (a matter to which we must return) will be necessary before he can read its meaning.

The sign given to the apostles was Christ: Christ as the centre of the whole covenant-history of the Jews, and its fulfilment; Christ as the centre of prophecy and miracle. The Old Testament can, indeed, only be fully understood in the light of the New. The Word of God incarnate gathers up and illuminates all words of God: he is the key to their meaning. But there was also given to them the gift of the Spirit, to enable them to grasp this meaning. In his appearances to his apostles after his resurrection, Our Lord in person 'opened their minds to understand the scriptures' (Lk 24.45). After Pentecost they would have the indwelling Spirit to enable them to see and understand: 'I will pray the Father, and he will give you another Counsellor, to be with you for ever, even the Spirit of truth...you know him, for he dwells with you and will be in you...The Counsellor, the Holy Spirit, whom the Father will send in my name, he will teach you all things, and bring to your remembrance all things that I have said to you' (Jn 14.16, 26). It is Christ that the Spirit is to enable them to see and to understand. These are the constituents of faith: God's Sign set in a manifold of signs that it is he who is revealing himself; and the gift to recognise and accept the message.

It is important to note that faith is a recognition of the messenger in the message. Christ is God's messenger, but he is also God's message – what God wants to tell us about himself, and about our relation to him.

A recognition *of the messenger*. Not any messenger would do. If God had merely wanted to give us some information, some truths or doctrines, another messenger would have done: if faith were to be primarily in propositions, these could, to

12

put it naively, have been fluttered down from heaven on pieces of paper. But he wished to give us himself. And faith reaches God, a person. Man believes when he finds himself confronted with God. This is the basic religious situation and experience.

But a recognition of the messenger *in the message*. We do not have any direct intuition of God's being: 'for now we see in a mirror dimly, but then face to face' (1 Cor 13.12). It is the same with our knowledge of a human person: we only 'get through' to the person, meet him or come to know him, through his words and actions, through observing him living. Thus in faith there must be some (not necessarily perfect) understanding of what God is telling us; there must be an intellectual element of comprehension, some grasp of *doctrine*, i.e. what God is teaching or revealing.

Now that may seem all very well for the apostles. But what about us? Let it be granted that they were presented with God's Word, or self-expression, in the flesh, and were granted the gift of the Spirit to recognise and acknowledge him. Do we meet Christ? The very historical links that join us to the apostles and the whole first generation of eye-witnesses seem also to cut us off. First, because we seem to have only a long chain of human testimony to rely on, and the whole force of the above explanation of the faith of the apostles rests on the fact that they were confronted by God himself in Christ. If we are not given their Sign, how can we have their faith? And, secondly, our faith would then appear to be at the mercy of scholars, forever sifting and revising the accuracy of what has come down to us from the earliest accounts, never able to give us any very reliable ground of certainty. Logically, the basis of our faith could be no stronger than the whole chain of human testimony and the whole apparatus of criticism.

To answer those questions fully would take at least two other books: one on tradition, showing that tradition is the handing on of revelation, and that revelation is always Christ himself, so that tradition is the handing on of Christ; the other to develop the whole concept of the Church that arises from these considerations. Here there can only be a general pointer to the answer.

Our Lord gives the answer himself: 'I am with you always,

to the close of the age' (Mt 28.20). The Church is the Body of Christ in which he lives, and it is precisely here that the answer to our problem lies. He lives in the Church and its members, to whom he has given the gift of his own life in baptism; in the sacraments of the Church he himself is the primary agent who sanctifies, coming to meet and give himself to each member of his body, especially in the Eucharist; he still teaches in the Church, as God's living Word. Hence, as the First Vatican Council declared (Dz. 3014, quoting Is 11.12), the Church is herself for us the chief sign, a beacon raised aloft among the nations. The Church is not simply a human reality, the end-product of a long line of merely human testimony; such a sign would indeed cut us off from the faith of the apostles. She is a divine-human reality, the Body of Christ in which he himself confronts us, so that we may be able to recognise him in his message, and acknowledge him. The Church can in a true sense be said to be the continuation and unfolding in human history of the incarnation. Thus, like the apostles, we are given a sign by God that is both divine and human. And, like them again, we are not merely given this external sign that is at once God's message and his messenger; we too are given, in the Church, the interior gift of the Spirit, 'opening the eyes of the mind' (Vatican II, *Const. on Divine Revelation*, n. 5) and enabling us to grasp the meaning of the sign, namely Christ himself.

Of course the position of the apostles was unique in the obvious sense that they knew Our Lord 'according to the flesh' (2 Cor 5.16), and that in them he founded the life and the faith of the Church. But it was not 'in the days of his flesh' (Heb 5.7) that they truly recognised him and understood his revelation, but only after the gift of Pentecost. And it was precisely *not* God's plan to live on in the world according to the flesh, but to do so in the Spirit, imparting his dead and risen life to his Body the Church.

In some presentations of the nature of faith, stress is laid on prophecy and miracles as particular signs (or 'motives of credibility') in and through which we are to come to recognise God at work, almost as if they existed independently and separately from the life of the Church. But, just as Christ

14

himself appears in human history in the whole context of, and as the climax and key to, God's self-revelation in the Old Testament; so it is the whole life of the Church, seen as flowing from Christ through the human centuries to our time, that constitutes for us the sign of God's saving presence and action. It is in the very God-like quality of her teaching, in her meaningfulness for human life, in the attractiveness and heroism of saints and martyrs in whom her life has flourished, in the immense goodness of her ordinary people, in her power to endure according to Christ's promise, where so many great human institutions have perished – in all these and many other qualities, which a few words cannot suffice to describe, and not only in more rare and remarkable events, that God shows himself at work; that he confronts each of us personally, and lays his claim upon us. It is traditional in Catholic teaching to say that faith rests on the 'authority' of God revealing himself. But the word has tended to acquire a small and legal sense in our language, and needs to have restored to it the dimensions of the Latin *auctoritas*, with its connotation of the 'august'. It is the very majesty of God that, in faith, we are enabled by the enlightening gift of the Spirit to see unfolded in Christ as the centre of God's saving action, continuous in human history.

2. *Man's Response*

Faith, then, is man's response to revelation – namely to God revealing himself in Christ (in his Church). It is the acceptance of revelation precisely as revelation. It is therefore basically a response of the whole man, and a single spiritual experience, not a succession of judgments and acts of the will. It can be called an affective knowledge, even a knowledge of the heart, because it is a response of the person of man to the person of God, and therefore engages and commits the whole man. It is not a merely intellectual or intuitional act of recognition or assent. In this connection, the whole passage from Vatican II's Constitution on Divine Revelation (n. 5) is worth quoting: 'The obedience of faith' (Rom 16.26; cf. 1.5; 2 Cor 10.5-6) must be given to God who reveals, an obedience by which man entrusts his whole self freely to God, offering 'the full submission of intellect and will to God who reveals' [a quotation from Vatican I], and freely assenting to the truth revealed by him. If this faith is to be shown [given], the grace of God and the interior help of the Holy Spirit must precede and assist, moving the heart and turning it to God, opening the eyes of the mind and giving 'joy and ease to everyone in assenting to the truth and believing it' [Second Council of Orange]. To bring about an ever deeper understanding of revelation, the same Holy Spirit constantly brings faith to completion by his gifts.

The passage brings out clearly that faith is primarily in *God*, and is therefore a response of the whole man, giving himself in return for God's giving. Because it is God that man recognises confronting him, his response can only be an act of acceptance, surrender, worship. However much he may have sought and struggled previously to reach truth, and to penetrate the values of life, by his own human powers, the totally different experience of confronting God must involve a sudden change from seeking to acceptance, from possessive desire to submission and surrender. Hence Paul speaks of the obedience of faith. Both in Greek and in Latin the word for obedience *(ob-audire)* is a compound of the word for hearing: not mere hearing, but heeding; submissive hearing, learning and receiving from one who teaches.

But God can be descried and acknowledged in this life only in his message: his self-expression is the incarnation of his Word. And so the Council goes on at once to speak of assent to the truth revealed by him. It is in one act, not in a succession of logically dependent acts, that man recognises that it is indeed God who is speaking, and accepts what he says. Our Lord said, 'I *am* the truth' (Jn 14.6).

3. *Faith in truths, doctrines*

We need to distinguish: the *genesis* or origin of faith, which gives an experience that continues through Christian life; the *analysis* of faith, such as we are trying to conduct in these pages; and the subsequent and separate *acts* of faith that we make in revealed truth.

We have so far been considering solely the origin of faith, and focussing mainly on the case of the apostles, or of one who comes to Christian faith from unbelief in adult life. But this original experience, which in the case of a child born in a Christian environment is not a sudden moment, but a growing and unfolding awareness, is 'original' also in the sense of being the source of a continuing state *(habitus)* in the believing Christian. It is the fundamental Christian condition or state, and develops with the development of Christian life. It is this basic acknowledgement or recognition that makes subsequent individual and distinguishable acts of faith (indeed, all Christian acts) possible.

The rather tangled analyses of faith that one tends to meet in manuals of theology seem to have got themselves enmeshed in complication, not to say confusion, by first focussing their attention on what is subsequent and secondary, namely belief in doctrines, faith in the abstract propositions, the intellectual content, of the Church's teaching. If I am asked why I believe what the Church teaches (doctrines), the only answer can be, 'Because the Church teaches it'. If I am further pressed with the question, 'Then why do you believe what the Church teaches?', the answer must be in terms of what has gone earlier in this chapter, namely that I recognise God-made-man confronting me in his Church; or, more succinctly, 'on the authority of God revealing'.

Substantially faith is simple. Abstract analyses of faith are possible, so long as one remembers that one *is* abstracting: one is singling out for separate consideration various aspects of a simple, and person-to-person, experience; one is not disentangling a succession of separate and dependent acts or experiences.

The Christian, then, can and does make separate acts of faith in doctrines, but only as products of a more original and underlying experience of recognition. We have noted already that the basic act of faith already has a doctrinal element, an intellectual content: it is an assent to revealed truth. But the

17

full deployment or unpacking in terms of human thinking of what is globally given to man in Christ, and accepted by him in faith, is an endless process. Human thought can never exhaust the content of what St. Paul calls 'the unsearchable riches of Christ' (Eph 3.8). It is an endless process in the life of the Church, which is ever deploying revelation (the total impact of Christ handed on in tradition) more fully in conceptual terms. The Gospel of St. John, for instance, or the Epistles of the New Testament, are already a theology – a more full thinking out of the message contained in Christ's life, death and resurrection, a message already set out in 'articles of faith' in the primitive proclamation (cf. Acts 10.34 ff., for example, or 1 Cor 15.1 ff.). It is an endless process, too, in the life of the individual Christian, who both by his meditation and by his Christian living is ever giving fuller expression to the values he accepts in faith.

When we say that faith is 'above' reason (i.e. reasoning), we are referring to the original and originating experience of being confronted with God in Christ: he is grasped as a person giving himself, a divine person who is beyond adequate human understanding; and it is only the special attuning of mind and heart by the Spirit that enables us to grasp him. This is not itself an act of reasoning, nor the product of reasoning; but it is nevertheless an act that engages the whole intellectual human person, and it therefore demands deployment or translation into conceptual terms. It is faith that generates understanding, generates theology. But the vision or grasp of faith can never be simply transposed into what is essentially the 'lower' key of conceptual understanding.

Hence the Church's understanding of her faith can grow, as it has done through the centuries in the development of her doctrine. So, too, can the doctrinal understanding of an individual grow. But a development in understanding is not necessarily a growth in faith, namely a deeper and more personal hold on God in Christ. The faith of the theologian is not *ipso facto* greater than the faith of the fishwife: the former may know more and more about God, but may know God – in the fully biblical sense of being attuned to him – less and less. Nevertheless, an educated person will need to think his faith more and more fully. This is at once a demand of his faith itself, a demand of Christ to reign as king throughout all the highest realms of human excellence and achievement; and a need of his own intelligence, striving to give to the content of faith the sort of intellectual expression that can live with and communicate with his other cultural patterns.

It is a pretty common, if not universal, experience nowadays that some time roughly between the ages of 17 and 30 a young person will experience a severe challenge to faith, which feels like and will often be described as a 'loss of faith'. It is partly due to the shock of emerging rather suddenly, at a time when intellectual powers are expanding rapidly, from a family environment in which Christian values are taken for granted into a world where they are ignored or treated as irrelevant. It is often partly due to the fact that, while cultural expression has developed fast in other spheres, the forms of expression in which faith is possessed, into which it is translated, have remained merely pictorial and immature. It is in any case a crisis process, in which a person's faith, hitherto drawn from and partly residing in a familiar environment, has to become decisively his own – his own personal response to a challenge that has been encountered and met. It is a decisive moment in the growth of the Christian person. Re-thinking will certainly be a necessary part of this emergence of adult faith. But, if what has been said hitherto about the essential constituents of faith is correct, more than a merely intellectual process is called for. God presents himself to me in Christ in his Church as a person, giving himself to me and at the same time summoning me: I have really to look at, to contemplate, the evidence of his presence and action, and this is the essential root of all prayer; I have really to descry and recognise the person of God, and not merely to have a tidy pattern of theories about him; I have to opt for him in a personal decision and engagement.

In all these processes of thinking the faith, one is involved in making acts of faith in the Church's doctrines, perhaps one doctrine at a time considered apart from others. In such acts the processes of intellect and will are more separable, and subject to consecutive analysis, than they are in what we have called the more basic or original experience and condition of faith. But such 'acts' can only arise from and be supported by the more underlying experience. In the subsequent or secondary act of faith, one can more clearly distinguish the functions of intellect and will. I find myself having to give intellectual assent to a proposition, the truth of which is not immediately apparent from ordinary human understanding of the terms and concepts involved. I choose to assent, and so use my will. But this process is only possible, and only saved from intellectual arbitrariness, by setting it firmly back and grounding it in the context where it belongs, namely my recognition of and commitment to Christ teaching in his Church. Hence the classical definition of faith as 'the assent of the intellect under the influence of the will' is open to some misunderstanding. It could be applied to the original experience of faith, as a way of bringing out that this involves the whole man and is not a merely intellectual process. But it more properly belongs to the secondary acts of faith that grow out of, while remaining grounded in, the fundamental experience.

4. *Faith and charity*

The distinction we have made between a primary and a secondary act of faith clears the ground for understanding the traditional treatment of faith and charity. The thomistic and scholastic classification of different virtues stems from an over-rigid distinction of various faculties of the soul, which came to be regarded as existing almost in isolation from each other: different virtues were perfections of different 'parts' of the soul. We are all familiar with the results for hagiography: a saint could be cut up into different chapters on his humility, charity, obedience, etc.

Without going too far into the matter here, we may observe that the fundamental distinction in the powers of the soul is that between intellect and will. Faith came to be regarded as principally, or even exclusively, the virtue of the intellect, charity of the will. One could lose charity (real assent to God, as Newman would have put it) by committing mortal sin, but one did not thereby lose faith (notional assent). On the other hand, one could not have real charity without faith, as the will by itself, regarded as separated from the intellect, is 'blind' and has no object to adhere to. Puzzles arose about the belief of devils! – and indeed about the faith of the man in mortal sin: if faith is an act of the intellect under the impulse of the will, is this latter not an act of charity?

Our analysis of the fundamental act of faith, however, enables us to see that it engages the whole man, and therefore his whole rational faculty, both intellect and will – not in subsequent or separable acts, but in a united self-commitment. It is an act by which a man 'entrusts his whole self freely to God' (Vat. II, above). At this level there can be no distinction between faith and charity. The distinction is more apposite at the secondary level, in the various situations we have briefly considered, and where the preoccupation or immediate object of attention is that of abstract truth or doctrine.

The eminence of hope, alongside faith and charity, in Christian tradition comes from 1 Cor 13.13: 'So faith, hope, love abide; but the greatest of these is love.' St. Paul, however, was not an Aristotelian, and his various lists of virtues are somewhat haphazard, as may be seen for instance from Gal 5.22, where *'pistis'* (both faith and hope, as will be seen later) occurs in the middle of a list headed by 'love'. His thought is not to be pressed into the service of Aristotelian assumptions about virtues or perfections. But in fact hope remains the Cinderella in this tradition, precisely because, with faith the virtue of the intellect and charity that of the will, there is no 'faculty' left for hope to be the virtue *of*! However, as will be seen in the next chapter, hope has a stronger claim to a place in Christian tradition than can be provided by a faculty-theory of the soul.

As a result of the intellect-will division, the word 'faith' in Catholic literature has a more strongly intellectualist flavour than it has in the English language as such. Other Christian traditions, and indeed philosophic convictions, have added their overtones to the word, with the result that it has, in common usage, anti-intellectual and even irrational associations: faith and understanding can almost be regarded as mutually exclusive, and there lurks in many minds a suspicion, if not a direct assertion, that religious faith is an irrational substitute for using one's brains. Hence one of the many difficulties of communication, when one discusses the subject with others. We will be further considering the rationality of faith later on. This chapter has tried to show that faith is ultimately in Christ – not just a person heard about; not simply as some vague and indefinable ethos; not principally encountered as a set of formulated propositions or doctrines; but discerned and acknowledged as God confronting me in his Body, the Church.

CHAPTER 2

SCRIPTURE

1. *In general*

Throughout the Bible God has a design for his People, and 'faith' is man's response to that design. The People of God see themselves as belonging to God's covenant-plan for them, and they believe in its fulfilment. So faith can be said to be *the* characteristic of Israel. To St. Paul, Abraham is the father of all who believe (Rom 4.11).

Greek religion does not contain this idea of faith, and consequently efforts to translate into either Greek or Latin the Hebraic attitudes lead to two different emphases:

1) Trust or hope *(fiducia)*, of which the object is God seen as reliable and trustworthy. Man, in his turn, must be faithful to God.

2) Faith *(fides)* regarded more as a movement of the understanding towards grasp of realities that God reveals by his word or by signs; the object of this faith is truth. But to the Hebrew mind 'truth' is not something as purely intellectual as it is to the Greek mind: it is opposed, not so much to error, as to the lie, to vanity and deception, to what lacks solidity and reliability.

2. *The Old Testament*

Faith in the Old Testament is mainly the trust or reliance given in the first of these two senses. The words used connote chiefly the solid and secure. God is the rock: one can rely on him, and have full confidence in him, but chiefly that he will fulfil the promises he has made to Israel. Old Testament faith, therefore, is mainly confidence in, a hope for, future events. But its perspective is that of this life: they are events that God will bring about for Israel in her future history.

But God did not make an unconditional promise. He made a covenant, and an alliance is a two-way affair: God will do his part, so long as man is faithful to him. The misfortunes that befell Israel are seen as due to man's lack of faithfulness to God. Faced with the manifold infidelities of Israel, the prophets came eventually to the idea of a Faithful Remnant, in whom God's promises would at last be fulfilled. Fidelity to God, i.e. man doing his part, came principally to mean faithful observance of all the details prescribed in the Law. Hence, man could trust and have reliance on God in so far as he was obedient and submissive to his commands.

God has his secrets, which he progressively reveals to man, but they are secrets about Israel's future history and greatness. This is not to say that they are concerned with merely material or political prosperity, for the saints of Israel looked for and longed for a time when holiness and justice would become established on earth. But their faith as such has not yet the idea of *fides* as a power of insight into spiritual truth or the manifestation of 'mysteries', in our sense.

3. *New Testament in general*

There are many 'beatitudes' in the New Testament, apart from the special list given in the Sermon on the Mount. And the first and the last beatitudes, spoken to Our Lady and to Thomas, are both about faith, and show the transition from Old Testament reliance-faith to New Testament insight-faith. Our Lady is called blessed by Elizabeth because she 'believed that there would be a fulfilment of what was spoken to her from the Lord' (Lk 1.45): this is Old Testament faith, a belief that God would carry out what he had promised.

There are many reminiscences and overtones in the New Testament of the reliance of the Old. In Gal 3.6-14, Paul argues that, just as Abraham relied on the former promise of God, so we (gentiles) rely on Christ and will receive 'the promise of his Spirit'. The faith of Peter, shaken by the passion, is a matter of confidence: once restored, it will confirm the confidence of others (Lk 22.32). In his lists of virtues, Paul uses 'faith' in senses that cannot be precisely defined by the context as either reliance or insight-faith. (For the hymn to faith in Heb 11, see Appendix I.)

The whole change of meaning in the word, and the transition to a new sense that implies not only reliance but new understanding, comes with the quite unprecedented fact that Christ claims faith in *himself* – not just as a miracle-worker, but as a messenger from God, and one who has power to forgive sin (Mk 2.5-11). He thus takes up the cry of the Baptist, 'Repent and believe': *this* faith involves conversion from sin, or, as so often in St. John, overcoming the world. Classic expression is given to the idea that faith involves a new understanding in the Parable of the Sower (Lk 8.9 ff.), where the seed is the word of God, and real power to 'grasp' this word is measured by [the sincerity with which men live.

But it is only after Pentecost that the full sense of the Christian word 'faith' develops. Before that, the apostles themselves did not understand properly the message conveyed by and in Christ; they did not understand that his kingdom, unlike that hoped for by Israel, was 'not of this world'. Indeed, the heart of the message was not there to grasp, until he had risen from the dead. They had been foolish and slow of heart to *believe*, and Christ himself *opened their minds* to understand. His miracles of opening the eyes of the blind were all along his chief preaching of faith, the clearest signs of the sort of faith he asked for. Indeed, all his miracles were such signs, and after the feeding of the multitudes twice with loaves and fishes, he could say to his followers: 'Do you not yet perceive or understand? Are your hearts hardened? Having eyes do you not see, and having ears do you not hear?' (Mk 8.17-18) He promised the Spirit so that they would truly understand. Hence, as St. John was to argue, true Christian faith was only possible after Pentecost.

4. *St. Paul*

Paul was 'seized on by Christ' (Phil 3.12) on the road to Damascus, and his blindness thereafter became Christian vision. Now his one task was to engender faith by the word of faith that begins as his preaching and then becomes the formula of the convert's acceptance (see Rom 10.8-17).

In the Judaizing controversy, where his problem is that of faith and justification (righteousness), it is mainly the reliance-faith of the Old Testament that he puts forward: we are to rely on Christ, in place of the Law, to open to us the way to the true promise: see Gal 3.6 ff., esp. v. 14; and Rom 3.3, 21-26.

A careful analysis made by scholars of the use of words for faith in the Bible shows that the characteristic New Testament use of the word is for acceptance of the proclamation of the Gospel: the early Christians have invented a technical and unusual expression for their faith, namely to 'believe in' or 'on' (Greek, *pisteuein eis*; Latin, *credo in*). The Gospel, spoken before it was written, is the proclamation of heralds: not an argument or a discussion, but a message of authority, which one can only accept or reject; acceptance of it is the technical sense given by Christians to 'faith'.

From various passages in Paul it can be seen that acceptance of Christ (belief *in* Christ) is more than a general reliance on his saving power and involves new knowledge and understanding. Thus, in Rom 6.8-11, and similarly in 2 Cor 4.13-18, submission to (confession of and obedience to) the Gospel of Christ involves acceptance of eschatological truths, belief in facts that are not seen. In 1 Cor 2, he explains at more length to his converts that faith in Christ leads to a new kind of spiritual wisdom: see especially vv. 6-14.

5. *St. John*

But it is above all in John that the meaning of Christian faith finds its fullest expression, as the central fact of Christ claiming faith in himself sank more deeply into the consciousness of the Church. It is a key to the whole of his gospel, which cannot be fully worked out here, that he is preoccupied with the theme of 'seeing' and 'believing' – between those who saw the signs only materially, and those who saw them spiritually and believed. Originally his gospel ended with chapter 20, and its

26

climax is precisely the story of St. Thomas: what Our Lord says to him is, in fact, 'blessed are they who have not seen materially, but have seen spiritually (believed)'. The theme runs through the fourth gospel from beginning to end: John himself is the one who reached the tomb first, and who 'saw and believed' (Jn 20.8). It comes out especially in the long chapter on the cure of the man born blind, with the irony of its conclusion:

'For judgment I came into this world, that those who do not see may see, and that those who see may become blind.' Some of the Pharisees near him heard this, and they said to him, 'Are we also blind?' Jesus said to them, 'If you were blind, you would have no guilt; but now that you say, "We see", your guilt remains.' (Jn 9.39-41)

The blind man came to see, not merely materially but spiritually: 'Jesus said to him, "You have seen him, and it is he who speaks to you." He said, "Lord I believe."' The Pharisees saw the same sign, but only materially: they were blind because they thought they could see.

More than this. The gospel was written for the Church which had not been eye-witness to Christ. It is precisely the argument of the gospel, not only that it is *possible* for the post-apostolic Christians to believe; they are in a *better* condition than those who lived with Christ and knew him only in the flesh. This is the point of Our Lord's saying to Thomas. Only after the Resurrection and Pentecost, in the Church, did the apostles understand, or see spiritually, the events they had witnessed. It was for this that the Spirit had been promised. It is the spiritual vision of Christ in the Church that matters, the grasp of the risen Christ in his glory. 'We *saw* his glory – glory as of the only Son from the Father' (Jn 1.14).

All the symphonic themes of his gospel are linked by John to the theme of seeing and believing. The thread of Light and Darkness that runs throughout establishes another connection between believing and knowing: the Word is Light; 'if you continue in my word, you are truly my disciples and you will know the truth, and the truth will make you free' (Jn 8.31-2); see also Jn 14.1-7, with its thread of 'believe ... know ... see'; 'he who believes in me believes not in me, but in him who sent me.

And he who sees me sees him who sent me. I have come as light into the world, that whoever believes in me may not remain in darkness' (Jn 12.44-46). One can link up other recurrent themes: to hear the word is to pay heed to it, to believe (5.25; 6.20; 8.43, 47; 18.37); this is the same as 'coming' to Christ (5.40 etc.), or loving him (8.42; 14.15-28; 16.27).

John puts his doctrine of Christian faith especially in terms of witness. Christ bears witness to the Father, to what is the Father's teaching not his own. He is the word of the Father, and light to those who receive this word. In turn, the Father bears witness to him: *outwardly* in the works he performs, which are miracles because they are signs (Jn 2.11; 5. 34; 6.27 ff.); but also *inwardly* in the witness of his Spirit (6.37, 44-46, 65; 17.6). Paul, too, speaks of the interior witness of the Spirit 'bearing witness with our spirit' (Rom 8.16). (Here are precisely the two constituents of faith that our first chapter emphasised.) Finally, the Baptist and the apostles bear witness to Christ (Jn 1.15, 34; 19.35 etc.), who himself appeals to the witness of Moses, the Scriptures, the Baptist. In his first epistle John points to blood and water, and the interior Spirit, as witnesses (1 Jn 5.6 ff.).

It was in meditating and commenting on St. John that Augustine drew the whole inspiration for his theology of faith.

CHAPTER 3

AUGUSTINE

This short book is itself very little more than a commentary on
St. Augustine, and to bring out the truth stated at the end of
the last chapter it is only necessary to give fairly fully one
superb passage from the latter's Treatise 26 on St. John
(PL 35.1607 ff.):

'Do not murmur among yourselves. No one can come
to me, unless the Father who sent me draws him' (Jn
6.43-44). Here is great store set by God's grace – no one
comes unless he be drawn. If you do not wish to go
astray, then do not try to learn whom God draws and
whom not, why he draws one and not another. Simply
accept the saying and understand it. Has God not drawn
you yet? Then pray that he may.

'What does the saying mean, brethren? If we are drawn
by God to Christ, do we then believe against our will?
Is mere compulsion at work, and not our own free will?
A man can enter a church against his will, he can come
to the altar against his will, he can receive the sacrament
aginst his will; but only willingly can a man believe. If
faith could be given by the body, then it could be given
unwillingly; but it is not with the body that we believe.
Hear the apostle when he says: 'for a man believes with
his heart and so is justified' (Rom 10.10) – and what
follows? – 'and he confesses [makes profession of faith]
with his lips and so is saved.' That profession rises from
the depth of the heart. Sometimes you will hear a man
making his profession of faith, and will not know
whether he believes. For to profess one's faith is to put
into words what one's heart holds; but these are mere
words, there is no profession, if heart and lips frame a
different creed. He who believes in Christ believes with
his heart; and no one does that against his will. Yet he
who is drawn would seem to be impelled against his will.

How, then, shall we understand the saying: 'No one can come to me unless the Father draws him'?

Do not think you are drawn against your will, for the soul too can be drawn, and that by love. Nor need we be afraid that men, who ponder words but are far from the things of God [one is tempted to translate this as 'linguistic analysts'] may hold these words of the holy gospels against us, and ask how we can believe willingly if we are drawn. For, I maintain, we are drawn not only willingly but with delight *(voluntate ... voluptate)*. What is it to be drawn by desire and delight? 'Take delight in the Lord, and he will give you the desires of your heart' (Ps 37.4). There is a certain hunger of the heart whose food is that bread that comes from heaven. And if the poet can say, 'each one is drawn by his delight' *(trahit sua quemque voluptas,* Virgil, Ecl 2.65), and if then there is no forcing but desire, no compulsion but delight, how much more truly can and must we say that a man is drawn to Christ who delights in truth, delights in happiness, delights in holiness, delights in eternal life – in a word, delights in Christ? Have the bodily senses each their pleasures and the soul no longings of its own? If the soul has not also its delights, how can it be said that 'the children of men take refuge in the shadow of thy wings: they feast on the abundance of thy house, and thou givest them drink from the river of thy delights; for with thee is the fountain of life, and in thy light do we see light' (Ps 36.7-9)? Give me a lover: he will know what I mean. *(Da mihi amantem: sentit quod dico.)* Give me one who has felt this craving and hunger, one who has wandered thirsting in this desert and gasped for the fountains of his homeland in heaven – give me such a one, and he will know what I mean. The cool and untroubled will never understand me. Such were those who murmured among themselves. And Our Lord said: 'Only he whom the Father draws will come to me.'

But why does he say, 'he whom the Father draws', when Christ draws towards himself?... The Father draws towards the Son those who believe in the Son precisely because they see he has God for his Father. For the Father has begotten a Son equal to himself. And so the man who can see, who can taste and savour with his faith, that he in whom he puts his faith is equal to God – that is he whom the Father draws to his Son. He whom the Father draws will say: 'You are the Christ, the Son of the living God.' Not as the prophets are sons, not as the Baptist, not as the holiest of men, but as the only-begotten and co-equal, 'you are the Christ, the Son of the living God' (Mt 16.16). See how Peter was drawn, drawn by the Father: 'Blessed are you, Simon Bar-Jona! for flesh and blood has not revealed this to you, but my Father who is in heaven.' There is revelation, there is God's drawing. You wave a green bough before a sheep and draw it on. You show some nuts to a child and he is drawn: he is drawn where he runs, he is drawn by desire, he is drawn without bodily force, he is drawn by a chain on his heart. If these things, then, that are among the pleasures and delights of this earth, are shown to those that desire them and draw them on – for it is true that 'each one is drawn by his delight' – shall not Christ draw us on when he is shown forth and revealed by the Father? What does the mind long for more than truth? Where will it turn its insatiable appetite, where hope to regale its taste with the flavour of knowledge, if not in the eating and drinking of wisdom, of holiness, of truth, of eternity?...

'It is written in the prophets, "And they shall all be taught by God"' (Jn 6.45). Why did he say this, O men of Israel? If the Father has not taught you, how can you learn to know Christ? All the men of that nation shall be taught by God; they shall not learn of men. And even if they hear men speak, yet understanding is given them within, Christ shines forth and is revealed within. What can men do who bring the tidings from the outside? What can I do now while I am speaking to you? I only bring the clamour of words to your ears; and unless he that is within

31

you shall reveal, what do my words avail? He who tends the tree is on the outside; God the creator is within. He who plants and he who waters toil on the outside – and that is our task. Yet, 'neither he who plants nor he who waters is anything, but only God who gives the growth' (1 Cor 3.7). This is the meaning of 'all shall be taught by God'. All who? 'Every one who has heard and learns from the Father comes to me' (Jn 6.45). See, then, how the Father draws: he delights us by his teaching, and does not draw by force. That is how he draws. 'All shall be taught by God' means that God will draw them. 'Every one who has heard and learns from the Father comes to me' means that God will draw them.

Here all the essentials of St. John's vision of faith are expanded: for faith man must be presented with the self-witness of God in Christ; but he must also be drawn to the truth incarnate, not only by the very attractiveness of truth itself, but by the interior witness of the Spirit; in faith itself he finds a new power of vision, which *carries its own guarantee* in its very 'delight'. The background of Augustine's approach to this passage of St. John is his constant preoccupation with the freedom of man under the grace of God.

In our first chapter we spoke of faith as an affective kind of knowledge, thereby appealing to a strong Christian tradition which runs through from Augustine to Pascal ('the heart has its reasons of which reason knows nothing') and Newman. Yet, for Augustine, the description is really too weak. For him, the search for truth was a passion and not a coldly intellectual exercise, the finding of it a total fulfilment. His heart had been restless for years in what he came to regard as a desert of inept philosophical speculation. The restless heart, searching for truth, could only be slaked by personal encounter with a God who reduced it to surrender. He would have had little sympathy with the 19th century Catholic insistence on the power of natural reason to reach truth by itself!

Still less would he have supported the view that human reason, philosophical and scholarly, must first elaborate an argued preamble or sub-structure, before it can reasonably give

the assent of faith. On the contrary: *crede ut intellegas*, he
frequently repeats, quoting Is 7.9. 'If all things have been made
by him, then understand that he himself was not made. If you
cannot understand, believe that you may (come to) understand' (*Sermon* 118.1, PL 38.672). And:

> Our Lord says: 'There are some of you that do not
> believe' (Jn 6.64). He did not say: 'There are some of you
> who do not understand'; but he gave the reason why they
> do not understand... they do not understand, because
> they do not believe. ...'We,' says St. Peter, 'have believed
> and have come to know'; not 'have come to know and so
> believed', but, 'have believed and [so] come to know'.
> We have believed in order that we might know; for, if we
> wished first to know and then to believe, we would be
> able neither to know nor to believe. (On St. John, 27.7, 9;
> PL 35, 1618-19.)

And again: 'If you have not understood, then I say believe.
For understanding is the reward of faith. Do not, therefore,
seek to understand, that you may believe; but believe that you
may understand.' (On St. John, 29.6; PL 35.1630)

Augustine, too, writes of the 'eyes of faith', for instance in
commenting on Ps 145(146).9: 'Do not envy sinners. You see
what they receive now: do you not see what is kept in store for
them? How, you may say, can I see what is not seen? Faith
truly has eyes of its own: larger, more powerful, stronger eyes.'
(PL 37.1897). This theme, taken up by Vatican II, when it
speaks of the Spirit opening the eyes of the mind in faith is to
be found in Ambrose – 'where true faith is, there is the true
grace of light', and, 'Christ enlightens us with the radiance of
faith' (On Ps. 118, *Serm.* 8.51; 17.8. PL 15.1316,1443) – and in
a passage of Leo (*Sermon* 27; PL 54.216), given in the Roman
breviary for January 1st, which deserves to be quoted for its
sheer latinity:

> *Cum ergo ad intellegendum sacramentum nativitatis
> Christi, qua de matre Virgine est ortus, accedimus, abiga-
> tur procul terrenarum caligo rationum, et ab illuminatae
> fidei oculis mundanae sapientiae fumus abscedat.*
> When we turn to understand the mystery of Christ's
> nativity, his birth from a virgin mother, let us banish

33

afar the gloom of human reasonings, and let the smoke of wordly wisdom roll away from the eyes of enlightened faith.

If the expression 'the eyes of faith' fell, early in this century, into some disrepute, that was because it had been transposed from its proper context into that of apologetic argument. It is not, of course, the contention of Augustine or of Vatican II that special interior illumination by the Spirit is needed for us to see the force of arguments which, if they are to stand up at all, must do so at the bar of ordinary philosophical and scholarly discussion; rather, that it is God, witnessing to himself in Christ, not the force of an argument, that the eyes of faith are enabled to recognise. For Augustine, *crede ut intellegas* means two things: A man cannot come to faith by human reasoning: he must first be given faith, and then alone will he find his reason fulfilled and satisfied. And, secondly, for those who already believe, there is a certain Christian understanding, a savour, a power of insight, which is capable of ever-increasing growth.

Finally, neither for Augustine nor for John is faith purely a matter of clear-headedness: rather, clarity of vision is a moral matter, and will depend on the way a man lives – a subject we will return to in our last chapter. So, for instance, he writes in *De agone christiano* (12, PL 40.299) that we must first submit to God in faith, and learn from him how to live in a growth of charity, and only then will there be spiritual insight into what was first taken on faith:

Wickedness is to love this world ... Such a life cannot see that pure, limpid and unchanging truth, and cleave to it and 'never be moved' (Ps 15.5). And so, before our mind is cleansed, we must believe what we are not able to understand; for the prophet's saying is a most true one, 'if you will not believe, you shall not understand' (Is 7.9 in the Septuagint version).

CHAPTER 4

APOLOGETICS AND THE PREAMBLE OF FAITH

St. Thomas Aquinas remained substantially true to the Augustinian tradition of the theology of faith, though his analysis of it in terms of the aspects of intellect and will leaves it a more bloodless diagram: the heart and the passion has gone out of it (for further details see Appendix II). But neither he nor any theologian for centuries to come was concerned with the later theological problem, What makes faith reasonable? And hence it is misguided to search his works for an answer to it. He lived in a Christian world, which was itself largely master of all human learning, and felt itself to demonstrate the *crede ut intellegas*. A purely secular learning, challenging the bases of Christian faith, was yet to come. But it is worth noting that he insists (e.g. *Summa*, 2-2ae.2.2) that, though different aspects of the act of faith may be singled out for diagrammatic purposes, it is itself a single and simple act, not a succession of acts. He lends no support, therefore, to later analyses which tried to construct faith out of a succession of such steps.

It was only in the 18th and 19th centuries that the idea gained ground in the Church, in the face of rationalist criticism, that faith needed to be grounded on a sub-structure of human argument, and could only be called reasonable in so far as it rested on such a 'natural' foundation: a clear antithesis to the position of Augustine, and indeed to that of the New Testament! And so we get the 'preamble of faith', the long body of argument, progressively gathered together in the single subject called 'apologetics', which starts by proving the existence of God and reflects philosophically on his nature, showing the possibility of revelation, and goes on to prove the fact of revelation in Christ and the Catholic Church by historical and scholarly argument.

Now it is in no sense the concern of this book to criticise the accuracy and intellectual solidity of apologetics. Let us grant as a hypothesis that it stands up. For our purposes the whole question is, what does it do? And a very vital distinction needs to be made. It is one thing for the Church, and it was vitally necessary for the Church in the 19th century, to demonstrate to agnostics that her faith, *which was already rational and reasonable by its own inner forces*, could in fact pass the scrutiny of secular learning. This is what apologetics is for, to demonstrate the rationality of faith, not to constitute it. The point is well brought out by Mgr. Léon Cristiani in his popular work, *Why we believe*. But it is quite another thing to state or to suggest that the Church must first provide herself with this full apparatus of apologetic argument, as a platform on which to rest her faith, before it can be called reasonable. The title of Mgr. Cristiani's book (in its English translation) is already ambiguous. Is this (apologetics) *why* we believe? No, as our first chapter has endeavoured to explain. But if the corpus of apologetic argument is called 'the preamble of faith', as in many theological manuals, then it is no longer being merely suggested, but is being openly asserted, that apologetic argument is the ultimate ground why faith is reasonable, and that it would not be reasonable without it. It is this position that we must submit to the following criticisms.

(1) The argument of the preamble appears to prove too much. It seems that we do not, after all, believe that the Church is God's appointed teacher: we prove it, and we would not reasonably believe her teaching otherwise. It appears that we do not even believe that Our Lord is God: we demonstrate this too, and could not reasonably put our faith in his teaching until we had done so.

There is no trace of any such attitude in Scripture, nor, indeed, in the Church's thinking until quite modern times. Our Lord asked his hearers directly for their faith, and blamed them for being slow to believe. St. John wrote his gospel, 'that you may believe that Jesus is the Christ, the Son of God, and believing you may have life in his name' (Jn 20.31).

It may occur to some readers as a theological difficulty to what we are asserting, that the First Vatican Council defined that 'God, the origin and end of all things, can be known with certainty by the natural light of human reason from (consideration of) creatures' (Dz 3004). A fuller account of official documentation must be referred to an Appendix, and here a few more general observations must suffice. The Council had to deal with two opposing tendencies: one that over-emphasised the powers of human reason, and denied the possibility or relevance of revealed knowledge; the other that was too sceptical (under the influence of Kantian philosophy) of human reason's ability to attain speculative truth, and gave a merely nebulous, emotional and irrational account of faith, as if to preserve it from critical attack. It did so mainly by reasserting both the genuineness and supernatural quality of revealed doctrine; indeed, assurances had to be given afterwards to those engaged in apologetics, who felt that the value of their work had been undermined; the Council curbs, rather than promotes, the opinion that faith, to be rational, must be based on an argued foundation. Its modified assertion about the 'natural light of human reason', which is in any case only about the existence of God, is understood of the inherent powers of reason, considered in the abstract, and not about the concrete condition of men. The encyclical *Humani Generis* was to affirm (Dz 3875-6) that, in view of the difficulties that beset him, revelation from God is morally necessary for man to attain even those truths of religion and morals, which human reason is inherently able to attain without it.

Vatican I also asserts the importance of 'signs' in God's chosen means of revelation, as making faith accord with reason. But it nowhere says that man, without the help of grace, can strictly demonstrate from such signs the fact of revelation (and where it is to be found) – still less that he must do this, before his faith can be reasonable. And we have given the fullest place to the sign-nature of faith in our analysis.

(2) What of the certainty of faith, if the preamble is the ground of its reasonableness? The string of apologetic argument is of a highly complex nature and includes many different kinds of study. There are first the arguments for the existence of God, and though 'metaphysical certainty' has an honoured name in some quarters, it would be very hard to disabuse anyone who maintained, even after a summary knowledge of the history of

philosophy, that there is nothing less certain (some would say, more misguided) than metaphysics. (Does our faith depend on taking sides *a priori* in such discussions?) Then there are questions of history and scholarship, and the interpretation of texts: about these, learned men have always been prepared to disagree. It is surely a sound attitude of any scholarly research, that an acquired position can only be regarded as a working hypothesis, open to be established or refuted by subsequent discovery. Do the arguments of the 'preamble' as put forward a hundred years ago look as sound today as they did then? And was faith in those times reasonable? One begins to feel it is a rather flimsy basis on which to rest one's faith.

But the real point here is not to suggest that apologetics of this kind turns out on inspection to be anywhere shaky or invalid. It is a much more relevant and important point. The reasonableness and certainty of faith, if they depend on the demonstrability of the fact of revelation, come to faith *from outside of faith*. Not only can certainty not be stronger than the arguments of the preamble: it cannot be of a different kind. Faith appears to be certain with only a natural certainty, such as can be provided by the branches of study that do service in apologetics. It would not generate its own, supernatural, certainty from inside. And any Christian knows that the certainty of his faith is quite different from that. It is not a blend of philosophical, historical and other kinds of certainty.

The same complaint may be put in another form. Why do we believe the truths of revelation? We would reply, on the authority of God who reveals them. But how are we convinced that we are in touch with the authority of God? If the answer is 'Because natural reason shows it to be so', then the whole of the assent of faith does not rest on the authority of God. The motive of faith becomes a sort of hybrid. The authority of God is invoked, not as a light to flood and transfigure the natural intellect, but in harness with that intellect's necessary contribution. The authority of God is no longer the self-sufficient motive of our faith.

(3) What holds for the certainty of our faith holds also for its supernatural quality. If the assent of faith is given partly, and

even fundamentally, because of scholarly operations, then faith ceases to be wholly the gift of God.

But there is more to it than that. How can faith be a gift of God at all, once the fact of revelation has been satisfactorily demonstrated? It 'stands to reason' that, if God reveals, what he says is true. It surely needs no special gift of God for one to reach the conclusion that his revelation must be believed? It is a mere evasion of the difficulty to reply that it is a big step from 'this must be believed' to 'I do believe', and that this (and this alone) cannot be done without a special gift of God. No doubt, to accept the truth of revelation may often be a step forward with immense consequences for a person's whole life; but we cannot equate the effort required to live up to one's convictions with the acquiring of, the assent of the mind to, those convictions. No doubt, too, that a great step is required for a mind that has climbed so far by its own powers, and learnt to depend on them, when hence it must submit to a higher power in the 'obedience of faith', submit to be taught and to be directed. It is a complete reversal of attitude. But is this all that there is of supernatural in faith? Is this all that needs God's special gift and assistance? Can faith be called supernatural only because God's help is needed for us to assent effectively to what we have already demonstrated to be true?

(4) The freedom of faith is closely linked with the question just touched on. If clinching proof is adduced that God has revealed certain doctrines, how can assent to these doctrines be henceforth free? The doctrines themselves have not, indeed, been demonstrated by examination of what they are about; they still have to be believed. But the fact that they are true has been demonstrated from outside. How, then, can the mind remain free to give or withhold its assent?

One must not overstate this point. There is certainly a difference between the mind being compelled to a truth, of logic or of mathematics, for instance, that has been clearly demonstrated; and, on the other hand, the sort of assent required of the mind to a truth that has not itself been demonstrated, and cannot even be fully understood, even though the fact that it is true has been demonstrated. One can see that the mind has a certain freedom to withhold assent in the latter case, which it does not have in the former. The point is, rather, that the freedom of faith is restricted to too narrow a compass. Have we only a certain freedom in accepting *what* God has revealed, and none in accepting *that* God has revealed? When we feel a bit shaky about some point of faith (and we must admit that we sometimes do), and then freely make an act of faith, we know from our own experience that we believe in God's authority and in what he is telling us all in one.

There is much more to say about the freedom of faith. But at least this much should be clear: the freedom of faith does not depend on being not *quite* convinced about some part of the proof for the fact of revelation. For, in that case, if one then decided to believe, faith would not be reasonable.

(5) The kind of analysis of faith with which we are dealing seems always to have in mind the adult convert, who arrives at faith after a period in which he did not possess it. And it must be noted that such converts, attaining faith after a long process of discursive reasoning, are rare: St. Paul and most others arrive by other routes.

But what of the faith of the simple and uneducated masses, who have never heard of the preamble, and could not understand and evaluate it, even if it were presented to them? What of the faith of children, who believe in a family setting, and with their father and mother? Is this 'simple' faith not reasonable? What, again, of the faith of the vast majority of educated Christians, who might wrestle successfully with the proof of the fact of revelation, if they had time, but have never bothered, or never had the opportunity, or have never felt the slightest need to do so? Should they have bothered, or is not their faith already reasonable and certain and free? Or is it only externally reasonable, because other people can provide a rational foundation for it? Indeed, what of the faith of the Church through countless centuries – was it, too, only reasonable because one day a rational basis would be worked out for it?

It would be a very great mistake to suppose that the faith of scholars and theologians, or of educated converts, is a more full or perfect faith, more endowed with the qualities proper to faith, and a paradigm from which the faith of other classes of persons is a declension in varying degrees. It is time to remind ourselves of our Lord's blessing on those who have not withheld belief until they have first carefully sifted all the evidence.

Nor may we imagine that the qualities of faith are distributed unevenly about the Church, as if the faith of the unlearned were more free and more a gift of God, and the faith of the learned more reasonable and more certain – and *therefore*, the suggestion would be, less free and supernatural. No, the faith of all is wholly God's gift, as it is also free and reasonable and certain. And if any faith should be taken as normal and normative, so that in it we can most clearly discern the qualities that belong to all faith, it is not the faith of the convert or of the theologian, but of the vast majority of Christians, among whose number most of us started, and to which all of us are proud to belong.

(6) Finally, the preamble of faith, in spite of its name, bears all the marks of a *post-factum* reconstruction: something elaborated by those who already had faith, in order to defend it, not in order to establish it. This does not count against the validity of the argument, as an argument: let it be considered on its own merits. But its origin is a guide to its true purpose – the defence of a faith already experienced as reasonable and certain and free. Many a man may have had barriers removed, and some mists cleared away, by apologetic argument, in order to prepare for the 'vision' of faith: and in that sense it can be a true preamble. But it is 'about' God. It can only lead, in Pascal's phrase, to the God of the philosophers. It cannot confront you with God, the God of Abraham and Isaac and Jacob, the living and true God, on recognising whom man worships and submits. And so it cannot, in any theological sense, be a foundation for faith.

And the view may certainly be contested that 'apologetics' is any particular body of argument, that can consolidate itself as a treatise or text-book and present itself as *the* preamble, in the sense of remote preparation for, or adequate defence of, the faith. Apologetics is concerned with answering the questions that people actually ask about the faith, or meeting the difficulties they actually bring. Our Lord had to defend himself against the charge of working miracles by the power of Beelzebub. St. Paul had to argue that Christians did not need to observe the Mosaic Law. Neither could be called very live questions today! The 'traditional apologetics' are in no sense traditional. For one thing, they are, in that form, entirely a preoccupation of the Western Church, and not seen to be relevant by Eastern Christians; nor is there evidence of their relevance for African or Asian Christians. For another, their shape belongs to a period of our own history which is already passing, or has passed. There is an air about the 'treatise of apologetics' of having nearly brought to perfection the definitive answers to the questions people asked in the nineteenth century! Today people simply have no interest in proving the existence of God. Those interested in the faith want the Gospel preached to them straight. If they do not believe in God at all, or are agnostic about his existence, they will not go step by step to faith: they will become convinced of God's existence, only in the very act of faith, when they find him confronting them, commanding them, and obey.

CHAPTER 5

FAITH IS REASONABLE

The task of this and the remaining chapters will be to hold up for closer inspection the main qualities of faith, which are already contained implicitly in the general outline with which we began. It is difficult to avoid a certain artificiality of treatment in thus dismembering what is in itself a simple and whole experience, and not a chain of experiences or a series of steps taken by the mind. Some of what is put in this chapter could perhaps just as well be put in the next. But the result aimed at is that by separate consideration of the qualities of faith the whole picture already given should be tested and, it is hoped, emerge enriched and clarified.

Our contention is, not that faith is reasoned, but that it is reasonable, a rational act. Nor that it is externally reasonable, but that it is rational by its own inner light and force. In considering this, we will need all the time to bear in mind that faith does not first evaluate a person, and then his message; it evaluates both at once, grasping the messenger in the message. We do not in this life have any direct vision or intuition of God; but we do meet and confront him in his self-expression. His message is at the same time the sign in which he gives himself.

Now, one constant factor in ordinary human faith can throw a good deal of light on the way God prepares our minds and enables them to recognise him – namely the 'interior sign' or the grace of the Spirit. As an example may be taken the faith a child has in his mother, instinctive at first, as befits the still undeveloped powers of a baby, but growing in colour and depth and content – and rationality – with all the concrete and personal contacts of unfolding life. It is not just a question of faith in 'what mother says', but the much more ultimate *faith in a person* that lies behind this. The parallel is close, because faith is not given primarily to a body of truths, but to Christ, known and experienced as a person with whom we live in daily contact in an expanding religious or spiritual life. We would not question for a moment either the value or the legitimacy of this faith of one person in another: the whole of our personal relationships are built of this very stuff. And the fact that this faith is sometimes misplaced and that we find ourselves deceived is no reason for asserting that it is never rational or valid or well-founded. We would hotly deny any suggestion that we could never be certain of another, however close we were to them. But if we try to analyse this faith in another person, we at once realise that it is built up out of far too many and too intimate and concrete situations and personal contacts to bear full statement: we could not spread it out before a third party in such a way as to provide valid evidence for him for our faith in that other person. Besides, any such statement of reasons or evidence would be wholly abstract and descriptive, whereas our own personal experience has been concrete, real, alive. We could only state a small part of the evidence from the outside, whereas we ourselves know that *in* and *through* and *beyond* any experiences we could describe, we have been able to meet a person – something, someone, unique and undescribable and yet the sole ultimate object and valid ground of our faith.

The constant and manifold experience of another person builds up in our minds a *pattern* of associations and linked insights. (The word is borrowed from Fr. M. C. D'Arcy, who analyses the concept much more fully in his *The Nature of Belief*.) In a unified and unanalysable form we carry our past experience of that person into our present familiarity, and it shapes, assists, and deepens our meetings with him and the appreciation of him which we derive from them. Composed of intellectual and affective elements of every kind, this pattern has prepared our minds for a more affectionate understanding of, a more loving insight into, that person as he presents himself outwardly in word and gesture and conduct. Outwardly he is many facets and manifestations, but we have learnt to know the inner and real self through this outward presentation; we have learnt the meaning of the signs; we can read them aright and assess them for what they really are, because the pattern in our own minds corresponds to and is sympathetic with them and enables us to see where they are pointing.

In the same way God prepares our souls by his grace to see Christ for what he is, to read the evidence for revelation aright. We cannot have a true appreciation of a religious value unless somehow there has been formed in us a spiritual pattern of soul that gives us eyes to see with. It may be that a child has been baptised and brought up in faith, so that God's initial gift is nourished by family and teachers and surroundings, with the co-operation of the child himself, until it blossoms into a mature and rich spiritual perceptiveness. Or the gift of God may be smothered by an evil life and leave at the most a bare and notional assent, a remote habit of mind scarcely affecting conduct and perhaps only persisting in so far as it is never severely tried or is barely allowed to occupy the forefront of the mind – persisting, it is to be feared, no longer as a virtue or quality giving the soul worth in God's eyes, but as a mark of guilt. Or God's gift may burst upon a man and hurl him from his saddle as he journeys to Damascus – though here it is possible to discern a great measure of spiritual preparation and psychological formation of the soul. Or, finally, God's gift may long remain latent in the soul of an adult, perhaps doing its work gradually and unrecognised for what it is, perhaps more evidenced by the way he lives than the formulas he recognises, until with apparent suddenness it blossoms into a full faith, and is taken for a stranger when in reality it is a familiar friend. 'You would not be looking for me, if you had not already found me.'

There are, then, more ways of being reasonable than one, more types of rational activity than are covered by the normal classifications of academic disciplines, such as philosophy, science, history. Our contention is that faith has its own type of reasonableness; that it is inherent to it, and that one should not try either to construct or to defend its reasonableness by going outside it to find support in other mental disciplines; rather should one try to describe and recognise that it is intrinsically reasonable. This is not a very surprising claim: how else could it be such a characteristic activity and experience of rational man?

But, even if it is not to be exactly equated with other types of rational activity, or made to rest on them, faith can be illustrated by other human fields of rational action; and in particular its own special type of perceptiveness and sensibility can be compared with moral judgment. It may even be claimed that we have here more than a comparison and illustration, and that religious faith is strictly a prolongation of moral judgment into an ultra-moral sphere; that faith is reasonable with just that type of reasonableness that belongs to moral conviction, though the subject-matter of the conviction is extended and the insight deepened, so that the source is reached not only of moral values but of all values. Clearly, faith is concerned with the way we live. Its subject-matter is Christ in his mystery – not just an eternal truth to be contemplated with speculative awe and reverence, but God's plan for our eternal destiny, for our life with him and the means of its attainment; something intimately concerning the whole fabric of our lives here and now, and the sense of values with which we shall view those lives. But faith is not only like moral judgment in that it is concerned with the value set on conduct (in its widest sense that includes our inmost thoughts, as well as external word and deed); the object of faith, like the object of moral judgment, is seen in the light of duty and obligation. The Christian believes, not merely because he sees it would be pleasant to believe, or ultimately advantageous or intrinsically valuable – he sees that it is his solemn duty to believe.

In a moral judgment our minds grasp an end or a particular line of conduct as both good and a duty. Honesty, kindness, courage – these all appear to us, not only as obligatory and compelling, but as desirable and admirable for their own sakes. It is not that we make any sort of inference – 'Because it is good I should do it', or 'I should do it, therefore it is good'. These are facets or aspects of a single and undivided apprehension. Moral judgment is the grasp of the compelling-good, of a value that imposes itself on us. Our moral sense, as the older type of British philosopher called it (though moral judgment is an eminently rational operation, and not a mere feeling) does not operate with any infallible independence, discerning the good from the bad and the better from the good by an unerring light of its own. A certain preparation of mind is necessary, if we are to make correct moral judgments, and as we develop in life our moral judgments mature in perceptiveness; conscience does not simply operate in isolation, and a man's whole philosophy of life will influence his moral convictions. Nor is moral judgment the imposing of an arbitrary pattern of values on reality; it is the discovery, as any intellectual operation is a discovery, of the values that are there; it is an assessment of evidence, leading to an assertion founded on evidence, and only a correctly formed mind will read that evidence aright.

In all these aspects religious faith resembles and continues moral judgment. Just as in moral judgment the object is not apprehended as a cold truth of purely speculative interest, like a theorem in geometry, but as a value, as something desired and loved, calling forth a response from the whole man in mind and will, heart and feeling; so, too, the object of faith is a supreme value, engaging and answering to the profoundest longings of the human soul. In neither case can the will (understood here as comprehensive of all the desiring and stretching-out side of our mental activity) be dissociated from the intellect, or brought in only at a certain point to impel to action. In both the true is grasped in and through the good *(sub specie boni)* in a unity of insight that cannot be broken up into a mere inference – that this is good because it is true, or true because supremely good. The insight itself can give rise to both these lines of thought, but it does not intrinsically consist in either of them. It is the apprehension of a value. A mathematical truth can lead to action by a separate step, in so far as we decide to put it to practical uses. But the perception of a value is itself an impulse to action; and, though it remains for free will to pursue that value or to turn aside, when it does accept the value by translating it into action, its force is that of yielding to, or throwing the whole power of the self and personality on the side of, a rational impulse and desire that already exercises a strong attraction – as Augustine so magnificently expounds.

Faith, then, is inherently reasonable, a rational activity of a particular kind. It is the admirable and necessary task of apologetics to show that faith does not conflict with other areas of human reasoning. But it is not this that *makes* it reasonable. Apologetics shows that it is *already* reasonable. Most of the difficulties, and indeed mistakes, about the reasonableness of faith come from a failure to be content that it should have a reasonableness of its own, and from the consequent efforts to reduce it to or to analyse it into some other type of mental operation. The same has often been done for moral judgment. If you could prove or justify moral judgments by a process of deduction from non-moral judgments, you would empty out their specifically moral character: e.g., if I should be honest ultimately because it served my best interests or ministered to the common welfare. So, if you could justify faith by any other means than that of its power to recognise God when he confronts you, there would no longer be any faith. One can only attempt to unfold what happens in faith, and thereby to make clear that for a special type of object a special type of awareness is necessary. It is very like our appreciation of other persons; it is very like moral judgment. It is not to be thought unreasonable for not having the reasonableness proper to scientific or aesthetic or mathematical or historical judgment – any more than any of these is unreasonable because it is different from all the others.

It is of the nature of faith, because it reaches insight into a *supreme* and *all-inclusive* value, that it should enlighten and assist the mind in all other fields; revealed truth throws abundant light on morals or aesthetics or history or the speculative problems of philosophy – or science itself. But the fact that it does do this, the fact that it can not only be defended by all these other studies, but can in turn correlate them into a more comprehensive understanding, does not constitute its reasonableness. It is simply one more external manifestation, one more encouraging confirmation, of the reasonableness that is already there.

Faith is reasonable, not reasoned. The grounds of its inherent rationality are in a sense private and incommunicable, much as our intimate knowledge of another person is something we cannot share, however we may try to give it expression by analysis and comparison. In that sense, the reasons for faith are valid only for those who perceive them, so that, strictly speaking, one who believes can only 'justify' his faith in his own eyes, not in someone else's. Faith justifies itself from within. 'Vicious circle', some readers may be exclaiming. But why should all circles necessarily be vicious? Charmed circle, if you wish. 'No one comes to me unless the Father draws him.' Another believer can understand, for he too sees God in the signs he gives of his authority and attestation. But faith is not fideism. It reposes neither on a hazy feeling of uplift or of unwarranted confidence, nor on an endless chain of authorities. It reposes on a vision of and insight into evidence, seen as a compelling value. I believe because I see I must, and because I see that my whole destiny is here engaged. No assent of the mind could be more firm nor more legitimately given than that in which man recognises his own destiny.

But that is only part of the truth, which puts it in too individualistic a way. Faith is always faith in and of the Church. And only the faith of the Church is perfect, undeviating, wholly comprehending – once one remembers that the Church is always a divine-human reality, and that through the ages the Spirit recognises and gives testimony to Christ in the Church. An individual will have faith at all only in so far as he shares, in his incomplete way, in the inner life of the Church and in the gift of the Spirit, whose fruit is the vision and contemplation of Christ. But his faith will remain in a sense only partial and imperfect, for faith is a virtue which can be possessed to a greater or lesser degree; it can grow and it can wilt; it is a gift of God that we must cultivate and which is destined to expand; a share in something too vast for us to possess fully. There may be a wholly loyal adherence to Christ's revelation in the citadel and inmost recess of the soul, but from there it has to spread and permeate the whole man. There remains something of the heretic in each of us until our faith has wholly integrated all our thoughts and desires; we are in part atheists, when we go about our ordinary work and pass judgment on men and events, as if we had forgotten God for the moment; or we are Pelagians at heart, when we attribute our spiritual insight and achievement to our own efforts and initiative. Furthermore, we may be more or less instructed in our faith. The faith of those who are ignorant (and we are all more or less ignorant) about

49

the very content of the faith – those who have the will and intention to believe all that Christ is and teaches in the Church, but have only the haziest idea, or even false ideas, about what he does teach – is in a way a reflected faith: it is a truly Christian faith, because it is faith within the life of the Church, and because at its roots there lies a firm adherence to Christ revealing himself in the Church; but it is an adherence of soul and spirit not adequately deployed or made articulate in the conceptual understanding.

Because faith justifies itself from within, we can say that the faith of all classes of Christians is 'equally' reasonable, without thereby meaning that faith in all such persons translates itself into identical, or even very similar, expression, whether pictorial or conceptual. We should have to mean this, if we were speaking of some philosophical system, and were affirming that its doctrines were shared by a number of adherents. But faith is not given primarily to doctrines capable of expression in a series of propositions. It is given to Christ in his mystery, who is incapable of adequate conceptual expression in any series of propositions. It is given to the person of Christ, who has become incarnate in human flesh and continues his life and manifestation of himself in all the life of his Church.

We must be careful not to equate the faith of an individual with the expression – pictorial, imaginative, poetic, 'mythological' – that he gives to that faith. In a sense, the delightfully vivid pictures of heaven and hell, courts of heaven and cauldrons of hell, naked men pushing up their gravestones at the trumpet's call to resurrection – in a sense this is what medieval man believed. But in a deeper sense it is not. As we have shown, it is always the messenger that is reached through the message, and the mode of expression man gives to the message is not the same thing as the religious perceptiveness, the lived experience of confronting and being at home with God, that gives rise to this expression. It would be inept to criticise the psalmist for saying the mountains skipped like rams, because of the possible disedification of geologists: the psalmist could well ridicule the critic, for not knowing the function of poetry. It would be just as inept to criticise the faith of children, who find Christ first in their mother and in their family. What more reasonable way could there be for God to reveal himself to children? And if they later grow in faith, and the expression of their faith matures, it is none the less the same Christ that they come to know and to express more fully, Christ who became vividly real to them from the beginning in that cell of the Church that is the Christian family.

We must be careful not to equate faith with its pictorial expression – or, for that matter, with its conceptual expression. Great theologians and thinkers have laboured through the centuries to translate the divine message that is Christ, given in the vivid and poetic setting of the Bible that is alone able to convey religious truth in its fullness, into better and better conceptual language, integrating it with cultural developments and thereby extending the sway of Christ's kingship over these realms of human achievement. But their faith, too, is the faith of the Church, as they are proud to confess; and it is not reasonable because or in so far as they have given it fit conceptual expression, or because they have established its relation to other knowledge. Their achievement, too, is but a manifestation, a further outward sign, of the rationality, the fully human value, that is within faith itself. Faith is reasonable because it is the seeing of God through the manifold sign of his majesty and authority; and the depth and power of that vision can be gauged by no intellectual standard, but only by the measure in which the life of the Church, the life Christ lives in our day and age, has penetrated and absorbed the soul of the believer.

CHAPTER 6

FAITH IS CERTAIN

That faith is certain is more a constant tradition of the Church than the object of any very formal pronouncement. The Church's professions of faith have always taken the form, 'I firmly believe', and the First Vatican Council declared that the believer could not have a sound reason for calling his faith in doubt (Dz 3014). Discussions of the matter tend to be in epistemological terms, and to be concerned with whether one can appropriately use the term 'certain' for the assent of the mind to truths which are not seen as true in themselves, but in their divine attestation. And if, at this level, some may feel that 'certain' is not a wholly appropriate term, we need have no quarrel, as long as the reality indicated by its use is recognised. For we have to remember, once more, that faith is not primarily given to truths, but to Christ, who claims an unreserved allegiance; those who give it, do so with complete assurance. For the purposes of this chapter, it is this reality which we will try to clarify further, and which will be indicated by the term 'certain'.

A correct analysis of the nature of faith and of its reasonableness, or even one that is merely on the right lines, should leave us with few difficulties about the certainty of faith. One can say that it is deeper and broader than that of any merely human discipline; one cannot speak of certainty as being more or less absolute, because the word itself denotes a definitive arrival of assent; and it is misleading to say that the certainty of faith is 'just as absolute' as other certainties, because this suggests that all certainties are of the same kind. The certainty of faith reposes neither on the self-evidence of the truth to which we assent, nor on the clear deduction of this truth from others that are evident. It reposes on the evident belief-value of its object; or, alternatively, it reposes on convincing and conclusive signs in which God reveals himself.

Once again the best illustration is provided by the faith we have in another person, whom we have learnt to trust with absolute confidence, because in and through innumerable and unchartable signs and experiences of that person's nature and personality we have come to know the person himself.

Further light can be thrown on the certainty of religious faith, if we look closer at two characteristics of it which are common to all types of belief, and which Father D'Arcy (in *The Nature of Belief*, chap. 6) calls 'interpretation' and 'the unity of indirect reference'. These two are closely allied notions. An example of 'interpretation' would be a medical diagnosis which is made, not as a consciously articulated deduction, but as a simple insight into the cause of a complicated condition: the patient exhibits various symptoms, and the trained mind at once 'puts its finger' on the cause. It is a power of seeing at a glance the relevance and bearing of a large number of different factors and details. Apart from strictly scientific instances, this is a type of mental operation which may be called particularly feminine. A woman seems to have a greater power than a man of noting detail and seeing a variety of assorted details suddenly fit together into a meaningful pattern. A sudden conclusion is thereby reached without any chain of reasoning, that can be laid before someone else, and a man will in exasperation demand 'the reasons' for the conclusion, or even call the process unreasonable and illogical, because it does not conform to his own more linear and more masculine type of reasoning or logic. This is delicate ground! We must hasten to add that the value of the illustration does not depend on whether this is a type of mental process used more often or more effectively by either sex. We all use such a process of diagnosis and interpretation at various mental levels, from the merely visual to the scientific and speculative. Detectives, at least in fiction, solve their cases this way; and we all have some experience of that sudden leaping to the mind's eye of the solution to some long-pondered problem. We would probably agree to describe it as a process of thinking, or of seeing, with the heart as well as the head. So in faith. An adult converted to faith will often say that, after long hesitation and uncertain wrestling, everything suddenly clicked into place – 'It was all there all along, but I just could not see it before.' Even in a cradle Christian the certainty is founded on (and the reasonableness consists in) a diagnosis of this kind, which includes a variety of detailed experiences in its scope and sees God's present authority and attestation as its point of convergence. Such an act of interpretation is hard put to it to give an account of its 'reasons'. The most that can be done is to give some kind of catalogue and description of the evidence, which will never be exhaustive, in the hope that an enquirer will be able to 'see it for himself'.

Of course, such a diagnosis can be wrong. But, as with any other type of mental process, the fact that it can sometimes be wrong is no indication that it always is. It cannot be replaced by some other type of mental process, and the only correction for diagnosing badly is to diagnose better. The wider the scope of detail on which such an interpretation is based, the harder it would seem to be to see the relevance and point of convergence of everything. But, at the same time, the wider the scope, the more assurance will the diagnosis carry, once it has been made. Faith has the widest scope of all: it is in principle all-inclusive, providing a new key to every problem and aspect of human life.

The notion of 'unity of indirect reference' is very similar to, and even overlaps, that of 'interpretation'. The point here is not that sudden insight with which we solve a complex problem but the way in which a vast number of assorted details, which we have never pondered *as* factors in a problem or as part of a jig-saw, support a conviction and generate its strength and firmness even without our noticing it. The classic example is Newman's one of our firm (and surely reasonable) conviction that Britain is an island, supposing we have not sailed round to make sure. Our assurance of any truth undemonstrated by ourselves would serve as an example, if it were of such a kind that sheer nonsense would be made of a great deal of our lives, if it were suddenly proved false. In the case of 'Britain is an island' our certainty ultimately rests on faith in the rationality of our fellow men and the reasonableness of their ordinary behaviour. For many men, their conviction of God's existence is built upon and generated by such a unity of indirect reference:

it may well be so for everyone's belief in God. We have been brought up to believe in God, and have found his existence corroborated by innumerable and varying factors – often at first appearing as challenges to our belief, but on assimilation strenghtening it – so that he has become something so fundamental to life as we have personally experienced it, that his non-existence would make nonsense of everything, the bottom would drop out of life and of rationality itself. The conviction is one that has thus been tried and tested continually in ways large and small, and has grown in strength and depth in the process, as it has shown itself adaptable to varying kinds of experience, and has proved not merely reconcilable with mature knowledge but fundamental to it.

In thinking of the reasonableness of faith, we have already briefly considered the faith of children and of the less educated, and similar considerations apply to its certainty. Christ wished to be continued and perpetuated in human life according to the real qualities and conditions of that life – refracted, as it were, into every cast of mind and every mode of life, so that not this individual or that but the whole body of redeemed humanity, the Church, should mirror the incarnation of God in human history. He wishes to reign in home life, peasant life, industrial life, professional and academic life. The faith of infants is, psychologically speaking, vicarious: it is their family who profess their faith for them at baptism, and it is in and through their family that they are attached to Christ in his Church. Hence a child's mother is to him the first sign of God's present authority; she is to him what the Church is to an adult; through her the child reaches God; and thus through her alone, as the first sign, can he reach all the other evidence of God's revelation. To the peasant, his parish priest and the Christian life of home and village *are* the Church, they are the all-inclusive sign of God's authority, the face which Christ presents to him.

Hence, as with the reasonableness of faith, we go astray if we try to evaluate its certainty, or question its legitimacy, by purely external and conceptual standards. God not only can, but does, reach the simple faithful through the ordinary structures of their life, and they are thus enabled to hold firm to him. Our Lord reaches a child or a peasant through signs that are of his making and are suited to a child or a peasant: and he even adds a warning that these things may lie hidden from the wise and prudent, if they persist in looking in the wrong direction. The revelation of God is a whole, and the signs of his attestation are a whole. But the face which this whole presents to each is individual, mediating grace to that person. It is only the Church that fully lives and reflects the Word of God.

But faith is not static. It is a virtue, that is, a form of lived human experience, the nature of which is to grow and develop. Just as Christ became man to incorporate all men into his Body, and founded his Church to spread to the ends of the earth, so it is the inner need of faith to expand in each soul and to reign throughout his life. As our human life develops, so faith must spread its grasp. Faith may be placid, in the sense that its security is not shaken, but it cannot be complacent. Hence, though faith is not of itself an assent to a system of conceptual expressions, the conceptual expression of our faith will need to develop, in order not merely to keep pace with, but to establish the reign of Christ in our own ever-expanding world: this, not by substituting knowledge of revealed truth for other types of knowledge or for their legitimate methods of enquiry, but by shining the light of revelation into and through these disciplines, and so integrating their findings in its light. 'In thy light do we see light' (Ps 36.9). This is the meaning of Augustine's *crede ut intellegas*: to understand our faith is to understand *with* our faith.

Christian faith, then, is on the move, mobilized: it has fresh worlds to conquer. And, on the one hand, when we actually live and experience this power of seeing in the light of revelation, we build up for ourselves progressively a vast 'unity of indirect reference', broadening, deepening, confirming our certainty. On the other hand, a new field of conquest will usually first present itself as a 'difficulty': for instance, a simple notion of the doctrine of papal infallibility will receive something of a shock, in the course of studying history, from the discovery of the varying fortunes of this truth in the unfolding consciousness of the Church. But, never founded on or constituted by the power of faith to answer difficulties, the intrinsic certainty of faith is not *suspended* by the encounter with such problems, any more than it is reinstated by their solution. Getting to grips with the difficulty, at the conceptual level at which it arises, we will emerge from the encounter with a confirmed faith that is deeper and wider, one which has taken possession of more of our world; we will have a more profound understanding of what papal infallibility is, and therefore of the whole nature of the Church. Faith, certain before the encounter began, will have found further confirmation.

'A thousand difficulties do not make a doubt'. We may openly agree that there is a certain tension and even struggle at the conceptual level of Christian thought. We may as well get used to the idea that there always will be, because there will always be more of the outer world and of our inner selves for faith to illuminate. So far from faith needing to turn 'a blind eye' to such tensions – as some seem to think – it will be endangered if we do not turn a very seeing eye to these problems. We will have introduced a half unacknowledged dislocation, and begun to drive a wedge between faith and real life. If we do not think our faith, indeed think with our faith, then it may well become remote and merely notional, slipping further and further back in our minds, not because its inherent power has failed but rather because it has not been used. But, on the other hand, as faith does not arise from 'solving intellectual problems', nor is it only nourished by tackling them: its basic nourishment is strictly spiritual or religious; it needs always to confront God in Christ, as person to person, and to live with him.

Some theoretical difficulties are brought against the certainty of faith on the false assumption that there is only one kind of certainty. One may agree that for any certain assent there must be evidence the value of which is beyond doubt; but this general condition can be fulfilled in a variety of ways.

European thought has to a large extent taken for granted a doctrine of certainty, having its roots in Greek philosophy, which fails to recognise this fact. In this view there is only one genuine certainty, that supplied by a formal deduction in accordance with the rules of logic, which is best exemplified in pure mathematics. The only genuine knowledge would be that derived by formal deduction from self-evident principles. Other states of mental assurance are recognised, such as moral certainty (e.g. that our cook has not put poison in the soup), and physical certainty (e.g. that the sun will rise to-morrow); moral certainty would be grounded on the rational behaviour of human beings, and physical certainty on the laws of nature. But such certainties tend to be regarded as declensions from and poor relations of formal certainty, and therefore to some extent spurious and not so certain. Ultimately this way of thinking derives from Plato's theory of knowledge and opinion: for him the paradigm of wisdom was to arrive by a long process of education at the contemplation of eternal and absolute truth; only from that summit to which he had laboriously climbed could a man look down on reality with really seeing eyes, and unfold what was now genuine knowledge in the form of a chain of deductive reasoning. The way up provided mere opinion; only the way down could be called genuine knowledge and could give absolute certainty.

Grand as this conception of knowledge is, it bears little relation to the many different ways in which our minds actually work. We have to recognise that there are different kinds of knowledge, and therefore different kinds of certainty. In studying history we can reach historical certainty, moral certainty in matters of conscience, physical certainty in the sciences; and the fact that we shall never have mathematical certainty in historical matters is no reason for thinking there are no historical certainties, such as the existence of Julius Caesar or of Jesus Christ. Neither the certainty of ethics nor that of science should be called any the less certain, for being different from the others. Of course, conviction can be misplaced in science or in any other field; but we can only correct historical judgments by better historical judgments, or scientific by scientific.

Some thinkers would wish to maintain that all certainties are merely formal, and concerned with the correct use of terms, whereas in any so-called knowledge we can never get beyond a sound working hypothesis, which of its nature is subject to revision. This is either itself just a plea for a very extraordinary use of language, which by normal criteria of usage would not itself be thought correct: are you certain that your father really was your father, or that your wife of today was the same person that gave you your dinner yesterday? Or it is the smuggling-in of a radically empiricist epistemology, which it is beyond the scope of the present book to criticise. Formal or mathematical certainty has, of course, a peculiar quality of clarity and firmness which is not shared by other certainties. But this derives from the fact, not that it is in any way more legitimate than others, but that it is concerned with so little of reality, and engages correspondingly little of the human make-up. Certainty in morals engages far more of the personality and correspondingly more of the world we live in: our will, emotions, desires, and not merely the coldly speculating intellect, are brought into play; the whole pattern of life may be at stake, or at least some far-reaching decision. Christian faith engages the whole of reality as object, and the whole of the human subject.

It is because of this simultaneous breadth and depth of scope that exceptional difficulties attend on faith, and yet it is for the same reason that it provides a supreme assurance: not supreme in its facility, but in the depths to which it strikes. When once the revelation of God is seen as the key to the whole puzzle of life, then conviction strikes home the harder for the power faith has to interpret so wide a design. For one who has possessed the key early, or from the beginning, faith will deepen its own certainty by the multitude and variety of the confirmation it receives, as the maturing mind progressively gives more adequate expression in ideas to the truth held globally from the outset, and relates this truth to the complex of problems and discoveries that developing experience provides. There will, then, remain – there must remain – a certain tension and vigour of conquest at this conceptual or educational level, which is itself a sign of the dynamic power of faith, and must never be considered as shaking the assurance which derives from, and remains at, a deeper plane. Nor must we look for any single and external measure of faith's certainty, as it exists in different individuals and different classes of Christian. To each and all faith is certain because it rests on a meeting with God in and through his created self-expression, a vision that leaves no option. Yet to all is that self-expression differently presented: part only of the whole pattern is spread before their individual faith, but a part moulded to their needs, which enables their faith, through its interpretation, to reach and to rest in the author of the whole.

It is because God himself is reached in faith that the assurance it gives cannot be a mere coming to rest of the intellect. Faith's certainty is kindled, not contrived. Just as, in examining the reasonableness of faith, we saw that will and intellect cannot be regarded as functioning separately or in succession, so with the certainty of faith. Here if anywhere mind and heart will fuse into a single act, for here the rational soul is presented with its ultimate goal, and its ultimate response is summoned. It is perhaps necessary to have felt the edge of the world's problems before the power of revelation to dominate them can be fully realised; necessary to have felt a certain weariness of soul with solutions that are partial, or remain in the realm of theory and of the abstract, and to have known that the soul itself bursts out of and overflows the earthbound or the easy answers; necessary to have known the need of some haven beyond which there can be no more seeking, or of some anchor that can tether us to the eternal and the ultimately reliable. It is in a person that faith finds its answer, by a person that the soul's assurance is engaged and held fast. Faith melts into charity and we surrender to one who will not let us go. *Da mihi amantem, et sentit quod dico*: give me a lover, he will know what I mean.

To sum up. A discussion of certainty is bound to be mainly in epistemological terms, and this chapter has tried to throw light on faith's certainty in these terms, notably by such concepts as 'unity of indirect reference' and 'interpretation'. But our contention throughout has been that faith, though it always involves belief in truths (message), does not basically come to rest in such doctrines but in God (messenger). Consequently, though faith must always have an epistemological dimension, it cannot be understood by exclusive reference to this dimension. Coming face to face with God is a religious experience that clinches in its own right, and this meeting itself generates an insight and a sureness of touch throughout the doctrinal realm. Let it be granted that faith in doctrines may be characterised by many hesitations, and has a dialectic of development which implies progress from a feebler to a stronger grasp. Hence, at this level the word 'certain' may sometimes seem inappropriate. Yet it is none the less true that the confrontation with God, which is central, remains fast and firm throughout the process of faith's growth, and of its nature spreads that assurance throughout life. Faith *is* a matter of life, and that is why it is so hard to convey what it means to any who are unfamiliar with it. It is bound to look different from the outside: from there its inner reality and intimacy, like that of family life or national life, can never quite be grasped, however fully it may be described. But if you are born and have grown up in Christian faith, or if you later come to find it as a home, then it is for you the very meaning of life, the basic, the ultimate, the most far-reaching conviction.

CHAPTER 7

FAITH IS SUPERNATURAL

Often in the course of this essay we have had occasion to insist that faith is a gift of God, and it is now time to examine more closely this quality of 'being a gift' which is an essential characteristic of faith. That, indeed, is what the term 'supernatural' primarily means: it is used of powers essential for man to attain the destiny that God has appointed for him, but which he cannot acquire by his own efforts, and so can only possess when and in so far as God gives them to him. All that we are in virtue of creation is already a gift of God, but to call faith a 'supernatural gift' of God is to say that it is in a further sense a gift, in some way over and above *(super)* the gift of the inherent powers of our human personality and make-up (nature).

On the analysis of faith here given there is no difficulty at all in showing that faith is supernatural. The Incarnation, the life-death-resurrection of Christ, is precisely that second, separate and gratuitous intervention of God 'over and above' creation, from which all grace flows. The central fact itself and its eddies throughout history are all grace, all supernatural, and these precisely are the signs and evidence that God spreads before us. They are more than that: they are the vehicle of his encountering us, person to person, and giving us himself. So, too, the testimony of the Holy Spirit in our souls is the further gift by which God enables us to recognise him in his signs. Thus, as we have explained matters, both outwardly and inwardly faith is wholly supernatural, whereas in the analysis based on approach from the 'preamble' the area reserved for the supernatural action of God seemed extremely restricted: his grace is brought in only as some sort of final, and not easily explicable, push, when cold reason has done its work.

The task of this section, then, can only be to deal with some difficulties that seem to arise about the supernatural quality of faith: they arise, we suggest, only through misunderstandings of what is meant by grace and the supernatural.

For instance, it might well be asked: How can faith be reasonable, if man's reason cannot by its own powers attain or exercise faith, but needs some special gift of God to be added to it? And if faith is wrought by God's grace in us, how can it be free? For, first of all, it seems to be insinuated into us from outside; and secondly, once the gift has been given, how can we be any longer free to believe or not to believe?

We must not be manoeuvred by such difficulties into an entirely wrong approach to the qualities of faith. It is not enough to reconcile the supernatural character of faith with its other qualities, or to show that faith is reasonable *in spite of* being supernatural. It is important to see that, rather, the qualities imply each other: that faith is reasonable, with its own type of reasonableness, *because* it is supernatural; free, with the kind of freedom proper to it, *because* it is supernatural and reasonable.

The fundamental truth we must grasp in examining the notion of a supernatural gift of God, the key to all the questions that arise about it, and the elementary truth so easily forgotten, is that we are dealing with an operation of God and not of man. God is creator. His giving, as any other divine operation in our regard, is creative. If for an instant we lose sight of this fact, and allow ourselves to regard God's giving as if it were a human activity, then immediately any number of false difficulties can arise. If some other human being were able interiorly to affect my mind, by some kind of immediate suggestion, then I should at once suspect any convictions that arose in my mind in consequence: they would not be really *mine* at all, because not produced by my own powers; and, because they were not in that way personal convictions, they would not be reasonable convictions. They would somehow be 'in' me but not 'of' me, mere parasites unconnected with my previous mental processes, and to that extent irrational.

But God's action cannot be equated with any such outside agency, whose operation would interfere with and impede my own powers. God's action is creative: creative at the level both of nature and of grace. At the 'level' of nature, by creating me God made me to be me: that is what my own individual and unshared personality ultimately reduces to – my dependence on God for being me. And it is crucial to this question of the supernatural to realise that any 'further' action of God's upon me, at the 'level' of grace, or over and above his action in creating me, can only make me to be more fully *me*. God 'graces' *what* he creates: he does not, in giving grace, interfere with, or revise, or cancel out his creation; rather, he fulfils it. To realise the creativeness of God's action is to appreciate that a supernatural gift to me from God cannot be the lodging within me of any stranger, or any intrusion on and interference with my own natural powers and functions regarded precisely as mine. God's gift can only realise my own individual and independent personality; it can only make me into an enhanced version of myself. Any gift, then, which God gives to my reason must wholly belong to and be part of *my* reason. And he who created my reason and made it to be what it is, does not by his further action make it to be any the less what he has already made it to be: on the contrary, God's giving of any added power to reason makes it to be more fully *reason*. Until we have grasped this truth we have not fully realised in what a full sense God's gifts are gifts – how fully they are made over to me and become my own.

We must, then, be careful not to set God's activity and our own natural activity in opposition to each other, if we are to understand what is meant by 'supernatural'. They cannot be conceived as two forces operating at the same level, and therefore as capable either of coming into conflict with each other, or of co-operating in such a way that part of the work is done by one force and part by the other. God creates. I am created. If, then, God enlightens the reason he has created in me, I shall be even more reasonable, with my own reason. Faith is reasonable *because* it is supernatural.

A further misapprehension to be avoided, apart from thinking of God's giving in anthropomorphic terms, arises from the term 'supernatural' itself. It inevitably suggests that the endowments and powers that are in us in virtue of God's grace lie within us somehow apart from our natural powers and endowments, as if the special vigour and sensibility afforded to reason by grace were not so much given *to reason* as a separate faculty or power in the soul overlaid 'above' reason and operating independently. With any such notion we are once again led to set reason and grace over against each other, and soon find ourselves asking how faith can be reasonable as well as, or in spite of, being supernatural.

It becomes necessary in some contexts to speak of grace as something 'over and above' nature and to use such terminology as that of 'levels' of nature and grace: indeed, use has already been made of such terms at the outset of this section, as a means of expressing one essential aspect of the relation between nature and grace. But by itself this terminology, and the idea to which it gives rise, is altogether too static in its associations, and needs to be complemented by a more dynamic one, based on the recognition that we are dealing with vital forces that are concerned with man's achievement and aspiration and affect the most vital energies of his soul. In attempting to supply such a dynamic notion we are deliberately going to couch it in terms that are as pictorial as those it is intended to complement. But as a corrective it may help.

We may imagine God, then, in the act of creation as setting the world and all the life in it 'out there', utterly apart from himself, a world of creatures set over against their creator. A tree or a flower fulfils itself and gives glory to God, by reflecting in its own measure his perfection 'out there', by growing, blossoming, fading again. The inorganic world changes according to strict natural laws. An animal fulfils its being, realises what selfhood it has, by living a span of life and coming to an end 'out there'; it is quite content to do so; it is made for that. But man is different. God no sooner sends him forth in creation than he draws him back again. Man alone of the creatures on earth is made for God, for a return to God, so that he alone does not fulfil his being 'out there', but only in this return. Certainly, man too has a span of life to live, but that span is not its own be-all and end-all. It is *also* man's return to God. The 'also' is important, because man's return to God is not a function separate and independent from his human life, a second journey unrelated to the journey of life. It is precisely in and through his span of life that he returns to God. And only in that return does he fulfil his own separate and unshared person-

65

ality. Grace gives *me* the only full *self*-realisation possible for me.

Creation, then, resulting in 'nature', is the action whereby God puts me 'out there' in being and sets me the conditions and framework of human life; the gift of grace, resulting in 'supernature', is the action whereby God draws me in and through human life back towards himself. 'No man can come to me, except the Father, who hath sent me, draw him' (Jn 6.14).

It is this notion of grace as, from God's side, a drawing of man back to himself and, on man's side, as a corresponding stretching out towards God, that gives us the more dynamic conception of grace and supernatural energies that we need. Within the terms of this conception we may say that the proper sphere of human reason is the framework and setting of human life 'out there' on the level of creation; its inherent energies precisely as a created form of life are concerned with and adapted to the living of a human span of life and dealing with the situations that arise within the framework of creation. And that is why the soul needs special energies and abilities to make the living of a human life to be *also* a journey of the soul back to God. It does not need a *separate* set of powers and energies, almost like an independent (supernatural) life clamped down on the existing one: the natural energies themselves need to acquire another bearing and dimension, so that what they perform within the framework of human life is also a response to God's summons and drawing-power. In giving us his grace God is not ultimately offering us a 'thing'. He is offering us himself, he is offering us a personal relationship. His gift itself enables us to respond and so draws us out of preoccupation with the created world; on our side we know his gift as at least the beginning of a movement of striving and aspiring towards union with him.

By so fashioning man that his destiny is nothing less than union with the divine life, and by drawing him towards that fulfilment, God has placed deep within the human soul at least the foundation and first stirring of a certain discontent with the world in which he finds himself, and an inchoate striving and aspiration beyond it. This germ of a new life may indeed be smothered beneath preoccupations nearer to hand, it may be consciously subdued, suppressed, stifled. But in his vision of beauty and goodness a man will catch a glimpse of a beauty that is comprehensive and ultimate, a good that is absolute and supreme. He will feel something of dissatisfaction with the world around him wherever he may look in it, and a growing desire for what is not limited and transitory. The attraction exercised by God may be shaken off and the gift it involves refused; or it may be yielded to, and in the yielding the new energy and aspiration will be intensified. For long, perhaps, a man may feel only the dissatisfaction and be unable to grasp or to state consciously to himself what it is that he is striving after. In this respect, divine faith may be regarded as both the beginning and end of a process. Faith is a beginning in that it brings knowledge of what this end is towards which one has been fumbling, and puts within one's hands the means to attain it; faith is not itself the attainment of the end, but henceforth the soul can stride out more confidently on its journey, knowing where it is going and how to get there, taking conscious and personal possession of the means which all the while God is offering. But to one who reaches faith in adult life it is also the end of a process: till its coming the soul has learnt to strive, but to strive in the dark, aware more of what is negative and dissatisfying, unable to see what force is disturbing it or what will satisfy its restlessness.

In drawing man back to himself and, in the act of drawing, giving to human reason the energy and ability to penetrate beyond what has been called its proper sphere, God is at once creating and responding to a deep demand of which he has placed the germ and foundation within reason itself. He is not, as it were, fastening on to reason an alien energy or placing within the soul by the side of reason an independent force, when he gives to reason the power to recognise as his own the signature he has written across his revelation, and to penetrate through and beyond those signs to a recognition of himself. One might say that it is natural to reason to recognise *that* God exists, by consideration and argument; it is supernatural to recognise God giving himself, and to respond.

Faith, then, is reasonable because it is an act of reason; it is supernatural because it is the development and fulfilment of a power that is only latent and unrealised within reason until God's gift of himself draws it forth and actuates it. But in this actuation reason becomes most reason, its own self is most realised and fulfilled. Once more, then, we can see that faith is reasonable because it is, and not in spite of its being, super-natural.

It should cause no great surprise or dissatisfaction if much should still seem mysterious in the relation between nature and grace, between God's creating and his elevating action. It is a matter that we shall expect to find mysterious, and in which, therefore, we can quite gladly accept that any exposition should have its limitations and inadequacies. But it is important to define and delimit the mystery in such a way that it does not give rise to problems that are false through being based on misapprehensions. The complaint may be made that all that has been done is to substitute a new paradox for the old: that it has been maintained that nature or creation is the proper sphere of reason, and at the same time that reason is most realised as reason and most fulfilled when God's grace enables it to penetrate beyond this proper sphere and guide us towards union with God. Be it so. Man *is* a paradox. His only actual end and destiny is union with God, and so there is deep in him an ultimate need of God; yet he has not within himself the means and power to reach that end and can only receive them as a gift from God – as a personal offer of union – as a gift, however, which, because it brings him fulfilment, makes him to be most himself.

FAITH IS FREE

There might at first sight seem to be a contradiction in asserting that faith is free and is also the work of grace. Either you are given the grace, the reader might object, and then you are given faith whether you like it or not; or you are not given the grace, and then faith is out of your reach however much you may want it. In neither case does it seem that you can freely believe or disbelieve.

Again, the analysis of faith criticised in the fourth chapter came up against the dilemma: either faith is reasonable and certain, and then it is not free – for one is not free to accept or reject conclusions that have been demonstrated with certainty; or the assent given in faith is free, and then the grounds of assent cannot be certain nor the assent itself any longer reasonable. The underlying mistake here, as we have seen, was the attempt to borrow for faith a type of reasonableness other than its own. There remains, however, from this dilemma the difficulty of seeing how the assent of faith can be free if it is also fully reasonable and certain. Here the reader might ask: When the mind sees the signs as manifest evidence of God's authority, and through the signs has a vision of revealed truth as a compelling value, how can the assent of faith be any longer free?

We must, however, not make a false start by trying to vindicate for faith an alien type of freedom any more than an alien type of reasonableness. And no more than in the previous section will we be content with a mere reconciliation. The aim will be to see what type of freedom a faith has that is also reasonable, certain, supernatural.

It will perhaps clarify the enquiry, if we begin by stating certain kinds or qualities of freedom which obviously do *not* belong to faith. The way will then be open for a more positive notion, less open to misapprehensions.

If I am walking along a pavement and find a pram in the

middle of it, I am free to walk round it either to left or to right – and it *makes not the slightest difference*, either to my present or to my subsequent fortunes, which I choose: the choice is made and passes without a trace. Obviously the freedom of faith is not one in which I am poised evenly between two alternatives precisely because neither holds any interest for me.

If I am still young and planning my future, I may find myself faced by, and poised between, a dull 'job' which seems to have excellent financial prospects and a really interesting career which, however, offers no chance of wealth and of the various advantages and opportunities that wealth would bring. Here my poise and hesitation does not arise from apathy. The choice will make a very considerable difference to the remaining course of my life. But even then it will not be a *comprehensive* choice. It may not affect my home life in its essentials; it will not radically affect my views and tastes, my standards of judgment etc. It is not an ultimate, an all-or-nothing choice, but only one among many big choices that will shape the emerging pattern of my life. But faith is such an ultimate. It cannot be ranged side by side with other choices, however momentous these may be, to collaborate with them, as part with part, to form a pattern of life. Of its nature it is architectonic and claims to engage, to shape, to evaluate the whole of life. Furthermore, while the choice of a career is concerned with the pattern of my earthly life, faith is a facing of eternal destiny; not the selection of one among many possibilities, but the option for my only ultimate destiny. All other choices are made between God's creatures; faith is a choice of God.

In choosing a career, or taking some similar step which will affect the whole of my life, I am to some extent gambling on uncertainties. I am launching myself into something of which I cannot know all the issue; to some extent I shall subsequently judge the value of the choice by its eventual outcome, and so I cannot in advance know, or know in full, the value of the choice. But faith is not free as a gamble is free, or as equally promising alternatives are free. In faith I am not taking a risk or avoiding a risk, but opting for a certainty. Once again the similarity of faith to moral action comes to mind. Faith is an act of virtue, a moral act, and in faith and the choices that depend on faith I can be certain of the value of my free act for its own sake, and also certain that it contributes to my eternal destiny. In faith I am certain of the outcome, and of the value of the outcome; whereas many a moral act (considered merely from an ethical standpoint and apart from all religious belief) stands alone and draws all its value from itself apart from, and even sometimes in spite of, its consequences.

We are inclined to look for the essential notion of freedom in the situation of choice between alternatives. But existentialist philosophy has made us familiar with a different idea, and theology can lead to the same conclusion. God is free. He is, indeed, the archetype and source of created freedom, so that our freedom must contain as its essential note some reflection and faraway echo of what is dominant in the freedom of God. God is free in his own inner and substantial life and not merely in his creative and redeeming actions. The Father freely begets the Son, Father and Son together freely give being to the Holy Spirit. And yet they do so necessarily. In the life of God, therefore, where freedom is most absolute, it is not opposed to necessity or founded on any power to do otherwise, but is opposed to any form of determination that is not self-determination. God cannot be compelled, or even impelled, from outside. More positively, freedom in God consists in absolute self-determination, initiative, self-possession and mastery of his own being and action.

Coming to ourselves, we know that in heaven we shall freely love God, indeed find in union with him the fulfilment and perfection of our freedom, as of all our being and personality. And yet we shall love him inevitably, without power to do otherwise. Again, the dominant note in freedom is not that of poise between open alternatives to neither of which one is committed, but it is the note of mastery and self-possession, the fully deliberate acceptance and engagement of ourselves in what we are and do. Here too we meet with the mysterious relation between grace and nature, which is such that grace (here the consummating grace of union) is so interior to myself as to constitute and to make me to be most fully myself, and so to fulfil my own self and not impose upon me something alien.

71

From the notion of freedom thus gained can be drawn a conclusion already contained in the examples given above of walking round an obstacle in my path or of choosing a career. Our freedom is not something that consists in an equal poise between alternatives, to be jealously guarded against any assault made on it by one object appearing more attractive than another. We are not the more free in our choosing the less attractive are the objects open to our choice. When a man devotes himself to some pursuit, to some career or cause of absorbing interest and inspiration, to some person whom he loves, his devotion is a free self-devotion: free, not in spite of the attraction of its object, but because in and through the attraction he is able to enter personally into the object and make it his own, and because his devotion is thus self-possessed, self-determined, mastered and owned.

A second most important conclusion to be drawn from this idea of freedom as mastery emanating from within the self is that we acquire freedom gradually. It is not simply something we have as a datum, a static and unalterable force or characteristic, but something towards which we are always tending and progressing. It is the mastery of determining and impelling forces that arise either outside the self or, within it, below the level of conscious and initiated activity. It is dominance and control, direction and determination of the energies which are stored up within the human person. Some degree of this self-determination is always there, though not always in exercise, or we would begin by not being free at all; but it strives and aspires to assert itself and to increase the sphere of its mastery both within and without the self. We win freedom by our efforts. To drift, even consciously and deliberately, is to submit to determinism and to be enslaved to it.

Now it is above all by faith that freedom is progressively approached and acquired. Whatever efforts we may make within the span and horizon of human life, there are many determinisms which we cannot turn to good account and make finally into something which we value: the broad conditions of our life, our basic abilities, the opportunities within our power of attainment, health, chance, inevitable failures – all these set strict limits to what we would like to be and to do, and there is no way in which we can transcend them. Evil, too, presses on us a sheer, brute datum, which we can only accept 'philosophically' and cannot ultimately amend or even seriously alleviate: physical pains and deterioration, the frustration of hopes, the loss of those we love, the sufferings of others, the sheer stupidity that often spoils what is beautiful and good. Only in the light of God's revelation can such factors take on a value and a meaning, and cease to be mere, adamant, facts that hem in and suffocate the best of man's endeavours. Only by faith can we master *all* our world, accept it all, make something of it all, not as an inevitable mesh of limitations, but as the very stuff of achievement – accept it actively and not merely passively, by taking personal possession of it and turning it all to worth.

Apart from the limitations to our endeavour that arise from outside ourselves, there are all the determinisms within. To drift along the lines of least resistance as they are dictated by the mere twists and turns of our own character, automatically and unreflectively, is no more free action than to follow blindly the lead and fashion of others among whom we happen to live. God's grace enables us to shape and take possession of our own selves; to be ourselves reflexively; not merely to 'have' certain characteristics and inclinations, but to 'be' our own selves, to make our own selves.

Faith, then, like moral effort, but further in its reach and wider in its scope than moral effort, is before all else a *principle of freedom*: it is a source of freedom, bringing liberation from the dark or blind forces of determinism either without or within; hitherto these forces stood over against us, menacing or lulling us; now they are ours to possess, to master, to manipulate. By faith we progress towards freedom. 'The truth,' Our Lord promised, 'will make you free' (Jn 8.32). So many converts to faith have for long struggled against the pull of God and fled him down the nights and down the days, in fear that submission to Christ would set chains about them and enslave their reason, only to find after all that faith liberates. It must be so, if faith brings knowledge of divine truth. For it is ignorance and error, as we readily recognize in other fields, that are the limitation of our abilities and their enslavement, cramping and marring our opportunities, whereas a break-through to the truth always brings liberation and power. How much more can this be claimed for the recognition of an ultimate truth about man, in which he comes face to face with his destiny?

This seems a good point at which to consider the question that may at many points have arisen in the reader's mind: If faith is God's gift, how can anyone be blamed for not having it? And if we cannot in that way be held responsible for our faith, how can it be free?

The Church teaches that no man can save his soul without faith, though she does not try to define what measure of faith God will require from each. The teaching implies, however, that one who dies without faith will be held responsible for that fact (if he has reached an age of moral responsibility). God is the judge, not we. We are never able to judge, even should we wish to, what has been asked by God of any particular individual, what graces he has received, how he has responded to them. Only in the rarest cases could we have any grounds for conviction that an individual has wholly turned his back on faith, and even then we cannot know of his perseverance in such an attitude.

But to return to the objection. When dealing earlier with the reasonableness of faith, and the ability God gives to recognise himself in the signs of his revelation, the impression may have been left that, when faith is acquired by an adult, the whole thing necessarily happens in an instant and by a single approach of God. The corrective, if one be needed, is to be found in what has just been said about our progressive acquisition of freedom, and also in what was said earlier about faith's being both the beginning and end of a process. In such a case the full gift of faith is not the first grace given. There may be faith, a fully supernatural faith, in God as a supreme being or as creator, or in God as somehow the source of man's destiny, or in Christ as a link with God, or in Christ as divine and as redeemer, before the coming of full Christian faith and the recognition of him in the Church continuing his redemption. There may be many graces, given and responded to, before the

74

soul has acquired even the most elementary and inchoative form of faith. There is a journey on which the soul voyages on the way to faith, traceable even in those like Paul or Augustine whom it seems to strike down suddenly. Hence we can at once see what is meant by a soul's being responsible for attaining faith. No grace is forced upon us: it is a gift that is offered, and it needs our ready co-operation to produce its effect. We cannot take the initiative and 'create' grace; but we can be responsible for its full or partial acceptance, or for its refusal. And only God can assess a soul's responsibility for the long series of graces that have been offered to it.

This gives us a further insight into the freedom of faith. It is a freedom that faith has because it is supernatural, because it entails a response to graces offered. Just as a man may responsibly lose his faith by neglecting it, or responsibly develop and perfect his faith, so he may responsibly be led to faith by his persevering acceptance of graces offered. We cannot discern the freedom of faith by merely regarding a cross-section of its history in an individual. The freedom of faith is not one of wholly having, or wholly not having, it at any given moment. Responsible possession of faith in one who has always had it, like responsible loss of or progress towards faith, is 'incarnate' in the long tale of choices that have made the soul's present state what it is. So, when a man has given half a lifetime to the acquisition of some specialised knowledge or skill, he is not able in a moment to lose all he has acquired: but it was freely acquired, and therefore freely possessed and exercised.

But is the freedom of faith sufficiently explained by showing that it can be freely acquired or lost? More than this has been claimed. It has been asserted that the assent itself of faith is free, in a way in which the assent to other perceived truths is not free.

There are two main things to say about this question. The first is that we must recall what has been found to be the dominant note in freedom, namely the mastery and reflexive determination by the self of its own act: not primarily the power to do otherwise; not primarily the power to withhold assent. It is, of course, true that while and in so far as I am seeing the signs as God's authentication and attestation, leading me to himself, I am not at the same time and in the same measure able not to see them as that. But it must be emphasised that it can never be possible, in faith, to stand in judgment over my beliefs, to pick and choose them, to adopt these rather than others for reasons external to the beliefs themselves. If that were the freedom of faith there could be no faith. Rather, I can only believe when I see my beliefs standing in judgment over *me*. It is precisely in so far as God himself is reached in and through the signs of his attestation that faith is possible. And it is precisely in that God is reached, that faith is free; as commitment to a person is always free. Christ in his mystery engages me and challenges me, and it is only with a full interior acknowledgment, a spontaneous act of self-giving, that I can respond to that summons and believe. Here again we can find considerable help in the comparison with our other personal relationships. Many a husband is so devoted to his wife that infidelity to her is simply unthinkable. Is his devotion therefore not free? We would rightly scorn the suggestion that this devotion was not freely given, was somehow extorted, or that a free devotion must somehow carry, behind the actual practice, a real poise and deliberation between fidelity and infidelity. It is free because it is a spontaneous movement of the self, an attitude of the self wholly adopted, canonised, possessed: it is in fact a gift of the self. So in the assent of faith. It differs from other assents to recognised truth in that it can never be just an act of the intellect assenting to compelling evidence: it must always be a dedication and gift of the self to the person of Christ seen and valued in and beyond compelling evidence.

We have argued that freedom is not something just given as a fact of nature, whole from the outset, but a power of self-determination that progresses towards an ideal in which the element of choice between alternatives is eventually (in heaven) wholly transcended; and we have therefore been unwilling that the freedom of faith should primarily be weighed by the presence of some power to do otherwise. Now, however, that the fundamental constituent of freedom has been emphasised, it is time to give due value to this secondary characteristic. For while we are still on the way towards the ideal and perfected freedom, there will remain a possibility of real selection, either because the objects for which we opt are created and limited and are therefore not all-inclusive goods, or because God, the all-inclusive good, is insufficiently grasped by us, so that even he can appear to us as an alternative set beside created things. There is in faith an element of vision and an element of reliance, of acceptance on authority; it is the latter which most characterises faith as a kind of knowing, and it is there because God can never be adequately proposed to or grasped by us. But we must remember that faith is of its nature transitory. It is destined to become more perfect and to transcend itself, as the element of vision progressively deepens and predominates, driving out the element of indirect apprehension, until in the final union with God, which in this life is never consummated though it is most nearly perfected in mystical prayer, there is only vision and direct awareness: the signs give place to reality and surrender becomes possession. 'For now we see in a mirror, dimly but then face to face. Now I know in part; then I shall understand fully, even as I have been understood. So faith, hope, love abide, these three; but the greatest of these is love' (1 Cor 13.12-13).

Until that time the object of faith is never sufficiently proposed to faith's vision, and there must always be an effort on our part to adhere to it as a supreme value. And this effort is the chief moment in faith's freedom: a supernatural freedom, entailing a vigorous effort of co-operation with God's grace, in order by its power to adhere to Christ in his mystery and to place him, in a whole-hearted dedication, beyond all alternatives. Faith is a virtue and has the freedom of a virtue. Whether attained in adult life by previous co-operation with grace, or present from infancy, it demands by its inner nature to be continually perfected. My appreciation of Christ in his mystery can deepen, as I yield to the pull of God's grace; or it can weaken. Faith can recede to the back of the mind, if I do not live up to it and seek to translate it into thought and action, relating it at every point to my real life. It is difficult to think that a merely nominal Christian, who scarcely translates his beliefs into action at all or even thinks of them, even though, when pressed, he would not deny anything the Church teaches, can be said to have 'more faith' than an 'unbeliever' who is sincerely responding to what grace God has given him. Without faith no man can reach God for whom he was made, for faith is man's adherence to and option for his destiny. But God draws every man to this destiny, and it is for God to judge what response he requires of, or gets from, each. We shall not reach God merely by failing to deny revealed truth, but only by a faith that is possessed reflexively and lived; only by a faith that looks to and gives itself to the person behind the truth; only by a free faith.

It was said above that there were two main things to say about the question we have been considering: the first, expanded to some length, leads us to the second. It was necessary to stress earlier on that the operations of intellect and will cannot ultimately be separated, and that it is essentially an act of the whole rational faculty operating in one: faith and charity together. It is, however, possible to single out and abstract for separate consideration the specifically intellectual factors from within the whole experience of faith, though it is then important to bear in mind that one is dealing with an abstraction, and not with the real act of faith. Now it appears that the objection we have been considering rests precisely on an abstraction of this kind: viz. the question, how, when we do see the signs as God's signs, can our assent to what they signify any longer be free? For, to take the intellectual factor by itself, the mind, since it never perceives the intrinsic truth of the doctrines to which it adheres, is always able to *think* the opposite: 'Christ is God' – 'Christ is not God.' Even while I believe and adhere to the first proposition, I am aware that my mind is capable of adhering to the second. I am in fact only able to adhere to the first by *setting it back* within the whole experience of faith from which it has been withdrawn, i.e. by making an effort to see it, not as manifest truth, but as manifestly attested truth. I am able to assert confidently that Christ is God only in and through the whole experience of faith, which is the recognition of a value that engages and compels my whole self, engages my love. The mind has to make this constant effort to see specific doctrines within their full context as a value recognised, and this effort itself is an index of the freedom of the assent so given. This factor, which any Christian would agree to be part of his experience, does not in the least contradict or mar the comparison drawn above with the devoted husband for who minfidelity is unthinkable. All the millions of Catholics, who would never entertain the least doubt about the validity of their beliefs or dream of suspending their assent, have still on entering a Catholic church to make a free and deliberate act of faith in Our Lord's real presence there. Such separable 'acts' are the product of a basic attitude of soul; but they are not an automatic product, as sensible vision is the result of opening one's eyes in daylight. They are a reaffirmation of faith, a re-possession and reflexive mastery of faith.

All these considerations show that faith is a principle of freedom, and is a moral matter, not a merely speculative one. The cry of the Baptist, taken up by the apostles, was that men should repent, be converted, and believe the Gospel. The demand that Our Lord made to the Jews, and that they were unable to meet, was ultimately for a new crossing of the Red Sea, a new decisive act of stepping out into their fulfilment as the People of God – namely that they should be converted from Judaism itself. To St. John faith is a turning from darkness that is not merely that of ignorance, lack of knowledge, to the light, and he sees this as a turning from man's sinfulness and limitation to God's grace. It is a liberation, as from the slavery of Egypt. It is rebirth. The whole of the First Epistle of St. John is really a commentary on this theme, that man must be turned from sinfulness to see the light, and that, reciprocally, the light that is Christ gives man the true vision. 'We know that the Son of God has come and has given us understanding, to know him who is true; and we are in him who is true, in his Son Jesus Christ' (1 Jn 5.20). So, too, Our Lord says to Nicodemus: 'He who does what is true comes to the light, that it may be clearly seen that his deeds have been wrought in God' (Jn 3.21). The thought is perhaps the same as that of St. Paul: 'Doing the truth in love, we are to grow up in every way into him who is the head, into Christ' (Eph 4.15).

The strangeness at first sight of the expression 'he who does what is true' is due to the hebraic opposition, as we have noted earlier, not between truth and error, but between truth and the lie. Faith demands that deepest of freedoms which is sincerity.

Faith is a gift of God – rather, God's self-giving, demanding man's self-giving in return. It is therefore supernatural through and through, and not only in some final step. It can only have the rationality, as it has all the freedom and conviction, of love.

> The act of faith is of its very nature a free act. Man, redeemed by Christ the Saviour and through Christ Jesus called to be God's adopted son, cannot give his adherence to God revealing himself, unless the Father draw him to offer to God the reasonable and free submission of faith. (Vatican II, *Declaration on Religious Freedom*, n. 10.)

OTHER SCRIPTURE PASSAGES

Blessed are the pure in heart, for they shall see God (Mt 5.8). This would at first sight appear to say the same as the passage from John at the end of our last chapter, 'he who does what is true comes to the light', and to be the clearest statement that faith will depend on the way a man lives. It is, however, modelled on Ps 24.3-4, which is about the freedom from outward and inward defilement necessary if we are to appear before God in the temple. In the Sermon on the Mount Our Lord is, certainly, stressing inner as against merely ritual or levitical purification. But in view of the eschatological bearing of the other Beatitudes, perhaps the first meaning of our passage is that purity of heart, or loving good and hating evil, is necessary to attain to the vision of God in heaven. So it can be deduced, rather than claimed as what Our Lord actually said, that good living leads in this life to a clearer vision of God.

The Epistle to the Hebrews is throughout an exhortation to faith and constancy, and in Heb 11.1 the writer appears to give a definition of faith, followed by a hymn in its praise.

The closest translation of Heb 11.1 would appear to be: 'faith is the pledge of things hoped for, the proof of realities that are not seen.' It is, then, rather a description of the effects of faith, than an analysis of its nature. The thought is in terms of the Old Testament notion of faith, as reliance on God to fulfil his promises: such faith, or hope, is not only an objective guarantee of future possession (because if we do our part, God will surely fulfil his), but is a demonstration of the existence of its object (as can be seen in the list of examples that follows).

THE ANALYSIS OF ST. THOMAS

(1) *The genesis of faith*

Augustine was a twice-born man, and his whole treatment of faith reflects the experience of his own conversion. Thomas Aquinas lives in a Christian world, approaches the question of faith on the more detached basis of his philosophical theology, and is less concerned to show how faith comes about than how it works; he is less concerned with what we would call the psychological aspects of faith, than with its analysis in terms of intellect and will. In some earlier works, however, he very clearly reflects the terminology and doctrine of Augustine. In commenting on the Epistle to the Romans, he writes thus:

> The first way in which predestination begins to be carried out is in the *call* of man (Rom 8.30), which is twofold. One is exterior and comes about by the mouth of the preacher (Rom 10.14) ... The other is the *interior call*, which is a special galvanising of the mind *(mentis instinctus)*, by which man's heart is moved by God to assent to matters of faith and good living. (Comm. in Rom 8.6)

> St. Paul writes: 'But they have not all heeded the gospel' (Rom 10.16): this he says to show that the word of the outside preacher is not a sufficient cause of faith, if the heart of man be not *drawn interiorly* by the power of God speaking ... So we must say that for faith two things are required: one is the readiness of the heart *(cordis inclinatio)* to believe, and this does not come from hearing (the preacher) but from the gift of grace; the other is specification of what is worthy of belief, and this comes from hearing. (Comm. in Rom 10.2)

These passages show various, and 'unthomistic', phrases for describing the work of grace in the soul, which at once recall the passage we have quoted from Augustine in chapter 3:

cor attrahitur interius virtute Dei loquentis; cordis inclinatio; vocatio interior; mentis instinctus quo cor hominis movetur. The use of the word 'heart' is, of course, taken from the passage on which St. Thomas is commenting: 'For man believes with his heart' (Rom 10.10). The *interior instinctus* also appears in the later work, the *Summa*:

> He who believes has sufficient inducement to believe: for he is led to faith by the authority of the divine teaching confirmed by miracles, and, what is more, by the interior touch of God inviting him. (2-2ae.2.9)

(2) *The analysis of faith*

St. Thomas's terminology is the basis for the later analyses of faith. But his differs from these in two very important respects:

a) He is explaining the functions of powers of the soul *in* faith, and is not trying to show how it comes about, still less to justify it at the bar of human reason.

b) He insists that his distinctions between intellect and will are abstracted aspects of a single and simple act, and not a succession of acts.

A characteristic passage is that in the *Summa* (2-2ae.2.2). For purposes of clarity it is here set out schematically, rather than written currently:

The object of faith can be considered in three ways:
1) as object of intellect:
   a) the material object of faith is what is believed *(credo Deum)*;
   b) the formal object of faith is that in which, or because of which, a man believes *(credo Deo)*;
2) as object of will (i.e. in so far as the intellect is moved to assent by the will): First Truth is object of will in so far as it is seen as man's end *(credo in Deum)*.

To the first objection we answer that these three distinctions do not indicate different acts of faith, but one and the same act of faith, which is related to its object in different ways.

A full commentary on this passage would be a long business,

for, among other things, there lies behind it the whole difference between Thomistic and post-Cartesian epistemology: for Thomas the intellect was not a mirror held up to objects to reflect their already constituted intelligibility, but an activity of rendering objects intelligible; there was no gap to be jumped between mind and its object. Hence the First (or divine) Truth is at once a light shone by God into the mind and what the mind dis-covers in the object: it is equated with the authority of God. The passage is at any rate worth quoting for its final insistence that mind and heart, intellect and will, operate together in faith in what is a simple act, not a process.

One further thing is clear from this sort of analysis, that Aquinas is here focussing his attention on what an intellect is doing when it believes in *doctrines* or propositions, that are neither evident in themselves nor fully understood. That faith is ultimately in Christ, he brings out in another passage:

> But as whoever believes is assenting to someone's assertion, what appears to be fundamental and, as it were, the end in every act of believing, is the person whose assertion is believed; and the things a man assents to, when he wishes to believe someone, are in a manner secondary. And so, the man who has true christian faith is holding by his will to Christ in matters that are truly part of his teaching. (2-2ae.11.1)

SOME DOCUMENTATION

(a) *Before Trent*

The Second Council of Orange, in the sixth century (Dz 371-397), dealt at length with the Pelagian and Semi-pelagian controversy, and was concerned to affirm two things: that faith is God's gift from its origins, and not a response by God to efforts initially made by ourselves; and that at the same time it is free. One passage in particular may seem puzzling:

> Even after the coming of Our Lord, the grace of faith is not just a matter of man's free choice, but is also conferred by the generosity of Christ on all who wish to be baptised (Dz 396).

The passage is not denying the freedom of faith, but asserting that it is *also* a gift of God. This is not the place to enter into the tangled controversies of those times about the relation of grace to freedom, but we may perhaps observe that the defenders of orthodoxy created unnecessary difficulties for themselves by thinking of freedom primarily in terms of choice between open alternatives, and not as self-determination, which can obtain even without consideration of alternatives.

(b) *Trent*

The Council of Trent was not concerned with faith as a psychological process, but as a necessity in the dogmatic context of grace, justification, predestination, and so was content to repeat the teaching of Orange. The Council was however concerned with the material object of faith, and condemned the doctrine that *what* a man is called upon to believe is that he personally is saved or justified: faith is not *fiducialis*, confidence about one's own salvation, certainty about it; nor are one's sins forgiven by this conviction that they are forgiven. The interpretation of one famous passage, which can therefore only be given in Latin, led to subsequent controversy:

> For, just as none of the faithful should have doubts of God's mercy, of the merit of Christ, or of the efficacy of the sacraments; so anyone, as he looks to himself, to his own weakness and to the imperfection of his dispositions, can have fear and trembling for his own state of grace, *cum nullus scire valeat certitudine fidei, cui non potest subesse falsum, se gratiam Dei esse consecutum.* (Dz 1534)

The main thing the Fathers want to say is that one cannot have a faith in one's own salvation that is infallible. If they had said *possit*, not *potest*, there could be no argument. But later theologians have sometimes argued that what they in fact say is that one cannot have the certainty of faith about one's own salvation, since faith cannot err; and that there is here a formal definition of the inerrancy of faith. One need not enter into the argument. It is not theologically allowable to take a conciliar statement and extract a formal definition from a phrase in it that is made in passing, and is not the central focus or object of the statement.

(c) *After Trent*

It was in the post-Tridentine period that discussions progressively arose about the analysis of faith. They are centred round two questions:

(a) Earlier controversies between schools of scholasticism about what makes faith supernatural: are supernatural acts supernatural because of their formal objects (in faith, the authority of God revealing)?

(b) The later effort to provide an apologetic foundation for faith, namely to prove by reasoning the fact of revelation. But then you are proving the formal motive of faith, the authority of God revealing. So how can the act of faith then be supernatural?

Our own analysis cuts the ground from under both controversies, and makes it unnecessary to go into them in any detail.

Both rest on unacceptable presuppositions. But the theological student may well wonder whether, in the course of these controversies, the teaching authority of the Church came out with any statements that make the viability of our analysis questionable.

For the reference of theological students, the chief pronouncements, some of very slight authority, are:

1. Condemnation of the views of Estrix (Dz 2119-21), who taught that natural evidence of credibility was essential for faith and measured firmness of assent.

2. Condemnation of the recommendation by Hermes of positive doubt as a necessary theological method (Dz 2738).

3. Bautain, going to the other extreme (and even daring to complain of the overrationalism of scholastic theology!) denied the effectiveness of human reason and made faith rest on a merely interior and emotive religious experience. He was made to sign certain propositions by his Bishop (Dz 2751-56), and some more by a Roman Congregation (Dz 2765-69). The main contention of these propositions is that reason is able to construct a valid apologetic argument; not that it must do so for faith to be generated or to be reasonable. Vatican I and *Humani Generis* were to recede somewhat from this position.

4. In the wake of Lammenais, Gerbet and Bonnetty criticised the idea of basing faith on apologetics (a view with which we can sympathise), but based it instead on the traditional consent of mankind, something external to faith itself, and were made to sign propositions vindicating the power of reason (Dz 2811-14).

5. Pius IX tackled the relation of faith to reason in his encyclical *Qui pluribus* (Dz 2778-80); the intention is to proclaim to agnostics the firmness of the apologetic argument that should lead them to faith; but the Pope does not say how the transition to faith comes about.

6. The treatment of Vatican I has been referred to in chapter 4. The Council certainly stated that God gives 'most certain signs' and 'proofs' of revelation, and in particular miracles and prophecy (Dz 3008-9). It leaves it open to one, however,

to hold that we encounter and recognise God in these signs, and does not enforce the view that faith, to be reasonable, should be reached by a process of argument from signs.

In picking one's way through these controversies and documents, it is important to bear this last reflection in mind; and also to realise that the focus is nearly always on belief in doctrines, and not on faith in Christ. We have never minimised the importance of believing in what Christ teaches in the Church, but have maintained that the puzzles that arise about faith remain insoluble at the merely propositional level. It is faith in doctrines that is defined by Vatican I as:

> A supernatural virtue by which, with the inspiration and help of God's grace, we believe those things that are revealed by him to be true, not because their intrinsic truth is manifest to the natural light of reason, but because of the authority of God himself revealing them, who can neither deceive nor be deceived. (Dz 3008)

It has not been sufficiently recognised that Vatican I opposes the natural light of reason to *revelation*, not to *grace*. Hence we were able to assert, in chapter 4 (1), that the Council does not decide about what human reason can do unaided by grace.

The encyclical *Humani Generis* (1950), while conceding that *revelation* is morally necessary for man, in the concrete limitations of his condition, to grasp truths of religion and morals that are in principle apprehensible by reason (see above, page 37), went on to insist (Dz 3890) that solid arguments for the existence of a personal God can be constructed by reason without the help of *grace*. This, however, is only to assert that such arguments are genuine philosophical arguments (for the existence of God, and not for the whole preamble). Nowhere does the encyclical suggest that a man's faith will be reasonable if and in so far as he can base it on such arguments.

MARTIN LUTHER

We are not here concerned with Luther's doctrine of justification by faith alone, i.e. without any value being attached to our good works, but only with the doctrine of *fiducial faith* attributed to him. In so far as this doctrine asserts that man not only can, but should, have an absolute certainty about his own salvation (and Luther constantly maintained this), it is condemned by Trent. However, this leaves something to be said on the psychological aspects of faith.

Luther's own religious experience was one of almost unallayed anxiety about his own salvation or justification. He felt such a burning need for certainty on this subject, that some have judged that he was morbidly preoccupied with it. This colours his psychological explanation of faith: what he is looking for determines what he will find. The whole point of faith becomes for him that his sins will not be imputed to him.

If some aspects of Luther's thought have at times been misrepresented, then even his greatest admirers would probably admit that this is very largely due to his own vehemence of expression. It is such a misrepresentation to say that, for Luther, the whole object of faith is one's own salvation. He believed, rather, in Christ saving him. And such a faith can rightly be described as a faith in a message seen in a messenger; it is not faith in a messenger without any message, or conversely faith simply in a message.

Luther's genius was religious, and he found in the religious genius of the Bible a solid ground of revolt against scholastic preoccupations with conceptual systems, especially the flimsy and sometimes frivolous scholasticism of his day. His whole battle against the institutional Church led him to minimise and even scorn the necessary role of the Church in transmitting revelation and in giving birth to and nourishing faith, and consequently to devalue doctrinal or dogmatic faith. All the same, it is true that faith is only given its full religious dimension when it is seen as a confrontation with God himself. On this particular point, we may say, Luther was right in what he wished to assert, and wrong in what he denied.

LOSS OF FAITH AND THE FAITH
OF THE UNBELIEVER

The assumption of this book has been that one can best understand faith by considering it at the centre of the stage, where the spotlight falls directly, rather than at the fringes or in the wings, where it is dimmer and mixed with shadows. The second half of the title of this Appendix is intentionally paradoxical: the unbeliever is one who has not got full Christian faith; it does not follow that he has not got a more rudimentary faith, even if he would not give it that name himself.

Every theological question tends to involve every other, and we are at once verging on the vastly complex subject of the 'salvation of the unbeliever' about which only indications can be given here. For a fuller treatment see No. 36 in this series, *The Theology of Missions*. It is an established part of the Church's teaching, based on Scripture (e.g. Heb 11.6), that there can be no salvation without faith. And the faith in question is that discussed in this book, faith in revelation. There cannot be another faith that has no connection with faith in Christ: for then he would cease to be the only means of redemption for men. But, whereas early Christian writers tended to assume that to be outside the visible Christian body was to be outside the means of salvation, the Church today teaches that 'divine Providence does not deny the help necessary to salvation to those who, without blame on their part, have not yet arrived at an explicit knowledge of God, but who strive to live a good life, thanks to his grace.' (Vatican II, *Constitution on the Church*, n. 16.) And the Council's *Decree on the Church's Missionary Activity* explicitly recognises (n. 7) that the help God gives must include the possibility of faith: and therefore revelation. Here we must lay aside the problem how revelation and Christ's grace can in fact reach such men, in order that they may respond to it by faith, and concentrate simply on the fact that there can be rudimentary or inchoative

Christian faith present among those who reject Christ, or even those who have never heard of him. In their own patterns of religion and even of good living they are searching for Christ and perhaps discerning him from afar.

This clearly has a bearing on those who to all appearances have lost the faith they once had. Our analysis has tried to make it clear that the ability to make the response of faith will to some extent depend on the way a man lives: and therefore, though the whole pattern of responsibility will remain one which we will never be able to unravel, we must admit the possibility of a culpable weakening, and a culpable loss of faith. But it is also clear, at the same time, that many who might be said to have lost their faith never in fact had a very personal hold on Christian faith: they may have lost only a mainly exterior attachment, which had never become that fully personal option 'by which man entrusts his whole self freely to God'. It does not follow that they do not retain a less coherent, less articulate, but none the less valid power of some personal response to the God they have discerned in Christ. Or it may be that a robust and adult faith may have been submitted to shocks which the person did not have full power to assimilate. This book has focussed on the mature faith of the Church. But who is to say how far that faith can extend its reach?

If bad living can culpably weaken faith to vanishing point, and the good living of the unbeliever conceal an implicit faith; then surely the good living of one who has apparently lost his faith without discernible blame on his part has an even stronger claim to be interpreted as incoherent Christian faith.

General works
  Henri Bouillard: *Logique de la foi* (Paris, 1964).
  Guy de Broglie: *Revelation and reason* (London, 1965).
  M. C. D'Arcy: *The Nature of Belief* (London, 1945).
  M. C. D'Arcy: *Belief and Reason* (London, 1944).
  Jean Mouroux: *I believe* (London, 1959).

On Scripture
  Joseph Bonsirven: *L'Evangile de Saint Paul* (Paris, 1948), pp. 177 ff.
  Joseph Bonsirven: *The theology of the New Testament*, (London, 1963) pp. 128 ff.
  Bultmann and Weiser: *Faith*, reprinted from Kittel's *Bible key words* (London, 1961).
  John L. McKenzie: *The Power and the Wisdom* (London, 1965), pp. 28 ff.

St. Thomas
  Chiefly: 3 *Sent.* 23 ff; *De Veritate*, 14 ff; *Summa*, 2-2ae.1 ff. For selected passages, cf. Thomas Gilby: *St. Thomas Aquinas: theological texts* (Oxford, 1955).

Post-Tridentine controversy
  Roger Aubert: *Le problème de l'acte de foi* (Louvain, 1950) gives a fully detailed account of the discussions of the relation between faith and reason.

Papal and conciliar documents
  For the Second Vatican Council the translation used is that in *The Documents of Vatican II*, ed. Walter M. Abbott (London, 1966).
  For earlier documents reference has been made to *Enchiridion Symbolorum*, ed. Denzinger-Schönmetzer (Dz) (Freiburg, 1965).

THEOLOGY TODAY

First published in the Netherlands
Made and printed by Bosch Utrecht